Devoted to Fishing

For Fishermen and Fishers of Men

Books by Charles W. Sasser

Nonfiction:
- *The Walking Dead* (w/Craig Roberts)
- *One Shot-One Kill* (w/Craig Roberts)
- *Homicide!*
- *Shoot To Kill*
- *Always A Warrior*
- *In Cold Blood: Oklahoma's Most Notorious Murders*
- *Last American Heroes* (w/Michael Sasser)
- *Smoke Jumpers*
- *First SEAL* (w/Roy Boehm)
- *At Large*
- *Fire Cops* (w/Michael Sasser)
- *Doc: Platoon Medic* (w/Daniel E. Evans)
- *Arctic Homestead* (w/Norma Cobb)
- *Taking Fire* (w/Ron Alexander)
- *Raider*
- *Encyclopedia of Navy SEALs*
- *Magic Steps To Writing Success**
- *Hill 488* (w/Ray Hildreth)
- *Crosshairs On The Kill Zone* (w/Craig Roberts)
- *Going Bonkers: The Wacky World Of Cultural Madness**
- *Patton's Panthers*
- *The Shoebox: Letters For The Seasons* (edited by)*
- *God In The Foxhole*
- *Devoted to Fishing**

Fiction:
- *No Gentle Streets*
- *The 100th Kill*
- *Operation No Man's Land* (as Mike Martell)
- *Liberty City*
- *The Return**
- *Detachment Delta: Punitive Strike*
- *Detachment Delta: Operation Iron Weed*
- *Detachment Delta: Operation Deep Steel*
- *Detachment Delta: Operation Aces Wild*
- *Detachment Delta: Operation Cold Dawn*
- *Dark Planet*
- *OSS Commando: Final Option*
- *OSS Commando: Hitler's A-Bomb*

*Published by AWOC.COM Publishing

Devoted to Fishing

For Fishermen and Fishers of Men

Charles W. Sasser

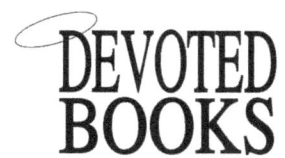

Denton Texas

Scripture quotations are taken from the Authorized (King James) Version of the Bible.

Devoted Books
An imprint of AWOC.COM Publishing
P.O. Box 2819
Denton, TX 76202

© 2008 by Charles W. Sassar
All Rights Reserved.

No part of this publication may be reproduced, stored in a retrieval system, or transmitted in any form or by any means, electronic, mechanical, recording or otherwise, without written permission, except in the case of brief quotations embodied in critical articles and reviews.

Manufactured in the United States of America

ISBN: 978-0-937660-44-7

For Mike and Kristy Curtis

Table of Contents

Introduction	9
SOLITUDE	11
PATIENCE	13
ADVENTURE	16
FORGIVENESS	18
SIMPLICITY	21
WONDER	25
REJUVENATE	27
FRIENDSHIP	29
PEACE	32
UNDERSTANDING	35
PRAYER	38
HEAVEN	40
GENEROSITY	43
SACRIFICE	47
DETERMINATION	52
MYSTERY	57
DELIGHT	60
COMPANIONSHIP	63
HUMILITY	66
LOVE	68
LOYALTY	73
FAITH	75
PERSEVERANCE	78
PRESENCE	82
WEALTH	84
THANKFULNESS	87
ETERNITY	90
COURAGE	94
BLESSINGS	96
PERSPECTIVE	99
TRUST	101
CONTENTMENT	103

DEATH	105
CURIOSITY	107
ABUNDANCE	110
HONESTY	113
SURVIVAL	117
HOPE	119
HUMOR	122
PRIORITIES	124
SELF-CONTROL	126
FAMILY	129
MEMORIES	132
Afterword	135

Introduction

When publisher, editor, and long-time friend Dan Case asked me to write this book in his "Devoted" series, it took me awhile to see the connection between fishing and lessons taught by Jesus in the Bible. Of course, like every Christian, even new ones like myself, I was aware of the metaphors the Bible employed about fish and fishing in order to teach its moral lessons. *"Follow me,"* Jesus instructed Simon and Andrew, *"and I will make you fishers of men."* (Matthew 4:19) But what special insights, if any, had a lifetime as an angler and outdoorsman taught me that might benefit other believers and those who might long to believe?

The more I thought about it, however, the more I realized that any special understanding or insight I had acquired in this mortal journey was either gained or sparked by my experiences in nature. Long before I devoted my life to Christ, I felt closer to God when I was on a creek bank or a river than I ever did in church. In fact, I refused to attend church for many years, knowing that my motive would have been like that of the Pharisees who prayed merely to impress men with their spirituality. Their actions were good, but their motives were not.

As a barefooted little hillbilly kid growing up in the Ozarks, I could most often be found down on some creek bank with a cane pole and a can of worms. I would lie there in the summer grass as night fell, gaze up into the stars, and I would wonder about the nature of all things, and about a God who lived up there somewhere in a place where it must always be summer and there were trees and streams and golden sunsets.

Many years later, in a canoe on the Yukon River, I watched a rainstorm skirt across my prow, followed by the most magnificent rainbow. It formed a perfect arch from one side of the river to the other. I remembered thinking it was like the gateway to Heaven, and I was about to pass through it.

I even accepted Jesus as my savior in the outdoors instead of in a church. I was almost 60-years-old and about to set a world's record by making the first transcontinental flight in an ultralite aircraft known as a powered parachute. The sun was just coming up and painting the earth 2,000 feet below in a soft patina of reds and yellows and early-morning blues. There was a ground fog in pastels and the mighty Mississippi River reflected back the rising sun like a highway of pure gold. Surrounded by such splendor, I prayed silently for God to show me the right way in life, if He existed. Suddenly, I just *knew*—and it was then I accepted Jesus as my savior. There I was, flying all alone high in the sky, laughing and crying and praying.

I know now that God has been teaching me all these years, using the outdoors as his slate. While I was fishing, I was also being taught patience and happiness, courage and friendship and inspiration, joy and humility, understanding and acceptance... What I would like to do now is share with you, in this little book, some of the life lessons I learned from God on creek banks. Even when I didn't know I was learning them. Perhaps, like Simon and Andrew, I might, through it, also become a fisher of men.

Charles W. Sasser

And in the morning, rising up a great while before day, He went out, and departed into a solitary place, and there prayed.
—Mark 1:35

SOLITUDE

My grandpaw was a dirt farmer who followed the rear ends of mules for more miles than I can contemplate. He would pause in the heat of the day while plowing, sweat dripping off the ends of his nose and chin to make tiny wet spots in the furrows at his feet, turn up a quart fruit jar full of water, squint his eyes against the sun's glare, and empty that jar with great relish. Excess water soaked the bib of his blue overalls all the way to his crotch. That old man enjoyed drinking water.

And he enjoyed fishing. Early of a morning when he was not working, he would tiptoe to my bed and wake me in time to catch the sunrise. "Get up, boy. It's time to go fishing."

Those were some of the last words either of us spoke all day. There was no need for conversation as that crotchety old farmer and I loafed in the summer sun on the banks of Vian or Sallisaw Creek and caught a tow sack full of bream, carp, and catfish. We simply propped our cane poles on forked sticks, watched our homemade bobbers on the surface of the water, and dozed in the midday when the fish stopped biting.

In the late afternoon, we pulled in our lines, hoisted the wet sack full of fish, and, still without a word, trudged home in companionable silence.

"The little shallow streams, you kin hear 'em before you ever get to 'em," Paw said. I called him *Paw*, he called me *Boy*. "The deep creeks now, Boy, the deeper they run, the quieter they are. They got more fish in 'em. More of everything. They don't see no need to chatter and go on all the time."

When I got older and came to understand more, I realized exactly what that half-literate but wise old man was getting at.

Quiet waters run deep and all that. People need solitude and silence in order to listen to their own souls, to explore life's meaning, to come to an understanding of existence, mortality, and their places in the universe. Several religious orders practice strict silence and emotional solitude while they probe the endless depths of universes within themselves in their search for God and meaning.

I've known people who practice various forms of Zen meditation with their legs crossed, thumbs and forefingers forming little O's, eyes closed while they hum and try to make contact with their "inner beings." Seems awfully complicated to me. All they have to do to find contentment and understanding, "the child within," is to wet a line and let the world go by. In silence, alone with themselves.

Of course, many people cannot stand the thought of being alone in a busy, crowded world filled with all manner of diversion and entertainment. Solitude literally scares them to death. My Paw would have called them shallow creeks. They always have to be chattering and bubbling, running hither and yon seeking something they will likely never find, too busy to ever know themselves.

"I love tranquil solitude," the poet Percy Shelley wrote nearly two centuries ago, "and such society as is quiet, wise and good."

Thank you, Lord, for granting me whatever wisdom I may have acquired in the solitude of Your wondrous works of nature.

Fishing Tip: Grow your own fishing worms. Build a compost pile in your back yard and keep it moist. Come spring, dig down into the compost for the fattest, juiciest worms that no perch or catfish can resist.

> *...And bring forth fruit with patience.*
> —Luke 8:15

PATIENCE

How poor are they that have no patience!
What wound did ever heal but by degrees?

That, of course, is from Shakespeare's *Othello*. I happened to think of that passage, along with similar admonitions from Jesus, while attending a reunion of my old army outfit. Good things come to he who has patience. *"Behold, the husbandman waiteth for the precious fruit of the earth, and hath long patience for it, until he receive the early and latter rain."* (James 5:7)

What brought these messages to mind was an exchange between two of my long-time army buddies who had gone with me on a recent fly-in fishing trip to Canada. Alan was showing around a photo of a trophy Northern Pike he had caught.

Donnie's lower lip protruded like that of a petulant child's. "Well, Alan might have caught the biggest," he pouted, "but I caught the *most.*"

Six of my oldest friends, including Alan and Donnie, had accompanied my grandson Cass and me to Ontario, where we caught a float plane that dropped us onto a secluded lake. It would return for us in a week. Our primitive cabin was the only one around for miles. The air was pure and unpolluted, the water clear, the forest pristine and unspoiled. We might have gone back in time to when God first created the earth.

This was my first fishing trip with Donnie. Extremely competitive and fretful, he had the patience of a child on Christmas Eve. *Patience? Let's go kill something!* He simply had to catch the biggest fish, and the most. He fished so hard that what should have been a relaxing outing turned into his own special brand of drudgery. Every evening when we all came off the lake for dinner, he conducted a quick inventory of fish caught that day. Should he find himself lacking, he immediately went back out to flail the water, sometimes long after nightfall while the rest of the group hugged a warm fire, had soft drinks, laughed and told fish stories.

Donnie had persistence. I had to hand him that. But there's a big difference between persistence and patience. Back when I was a kid and lost patience from not catching fish, Paw would half-smile and say, "You're not holding your mouth right."

I practiced holding my mouth different ways. Eventually, I understood that I shouldn't take him literally. He was teaching me patience. I relaxed, enjoyed the moment—and, sure enough, good things come to he who waits.

Those who are merely persistent without patience often fail to recognize good things even when they do come. Never satisfied, they must continue to test themselves against others, rarely ever acquiring the joy and contentment of those who have learned true patience.

My friend Darrell Turner—whom I call "D" and who was also along on the trip—and I have fished together for many years: teasing rainbow trout in the Red River in Arkansas, trot lining tributaries off Keystone Lake in Oklahoma, jigging for walleye in Canada, spin fishing for grayling in Alaska. A man of goodness, Godliness and unlimited patience, he can fish all day, catch nothing, and still consider the day productive and well spent.

"You don't have to catch something to have a good day," he says. "It's reward enough to enjoy nature's beauty."

Fishing is an exercise in patience that extends into all other areas of life. I look around at modern culture with all its frantic rushing back and forth and wonder what has happened to us. We are obsessed with what I call the Cult of Immediate Gratification. *I want mine, and I want it now!* Like an adolescent in the toy department at Wal-Mart throwing a fit over a new bicycle.

"Christmas is almost here," parents protest.

"No! I want it *now!*"

No one wants to start at the bottom of his profession and work to the top. A college grad expects to start out as CEO. Newly-married young couples go into hock for houses they cannot afford. Junior insists daddy buy him a new car as soon as he turns sixteen.

My grandson Cass turned sixteen and begged his dad to build him a little apartment. A room of his own wasn't enough.

"I didn't have my own *bed* until I went into the military," I chastised him. I slept with my two brothers. Our parents couldn't afford another bed.

A recent poll asked a broad group of respondents how they thought most rich people became that way. Guess what? Work, which is the correct answer, and which, incidentally, requires patience, appeared at the bottom of the poll results. The favorite responses, predictably, reflected modern society's *I want mine NOW* mentality: You either inherited wealth, or you won the lottery.

What these people need is to go fishing.

Though I sometimes lack patience, Lord, I realize that it is a quality taught by You as we await Your return.

Fishing Tip: For night fishing—or when you prefer to take a nap in the sun—a tiny bell rigged to the end of your bait casting rod will alert you when Ol' Whiskers takes a big bite.

> *And God said unto them, Be fruitful, and multiply, and replenish the earth, and subdue it: and have dominion over the fish of the sea, and over the fowl of the air, and over every living thing that moveth upon the earth.*
> —Genesis 1:28

ADVENTURE

If ever you doubt whether or not God loves wildness and adventure, all you have to do is spend the night camped alone in a wilderness, canoe white water, fly an ultralite over a mountain, kill and eat a rattlesnake, swim with sharks...

Richard Ray's thought that Sir Frances Drake the pirate had scuttled a treasure ship in shallow water off the Pacific coast of Costa Rica. Richard, perhaps the most successful treasure hunter in the world, and I and several associates were SCUBA-diving in Drake's Bay searching for the long-lost vessel.

One afternoon on a dive, I spotted a six-foot-long blacktip shark threading its way casually between the banks of an underwater stream about fifty feet below me in clear water. Surprisingly enough, a diver rarely encounters sharks; I had seen a nurse shark or mud shark a few times during my years of diving, but had never swam with a "man eater." I couldn't resist the opportunity.

My dive partner shook his head frantically to dissuade me, but, ignoring him, I flipped my fins and dived straight down toward the beautiful big fish. It continued to swim nonchalantly along the streambed, its eyes lifeless and cobra-like, jaws slightly parted so that I could see its teeth.

I came in behind, swimming hard to overtake. It increased its speed. Soon, I was chasing the big fish in an exhilarating game of tag. Maybe the poor shark thought I was going to eat *it*.

Exhausted, I fell behind. The blacktip vanished into deeper

water with a final flip of its tail. Swimming to near the surface, I slowly returned to where I had abandoned my partner. I spotted him about thirty feet below me. I could tell he hadn't seen which way I went and was nervous about it. I couldn't resist the temptation.

I dived straight down along his bubbles and thrust my head around directly into his downward-looking face. His eyes bulged and he gasped and back-swam, like a dolphin tail walking. He thought the shark had him. Both of us nearly drowned, he from alarm, me from laughing through my mask and mouthpiece.

A man cannot live simply to keep his fingernails clean. A boy seldom dreams of being sensitive, soft, manageable, and, well, feminine. God meant it that way. Didn't he charge Adam with replenishing the earth and subduing it? The male of our species needs to go where his soul cannot be folded, spindled, or mutilated. All men die; few men ever really live.

"Adventure, with all its requisite danger and wildness, is a deeply spiritual longing written into the soul of man," John Eldridge wrote in *Wild At Heart.* "The masculine heart needs a place where nothing is prefabricated, modular, nonfat, ziplock, franchised, on-line, microwavable. Where there are no deadlines, cell phones, or committee meetings... A man needs to feel the rhythm of the earth, he needs to have a hand in something real—the tiller of a boat, a set or reins, the roughness of a rope..."

From the beginning of my life here on Earth, dear God, You have encouraged me to live the way Adam was meant to live, to explore and to cherish Your magnificent creations in all aspects, with the ultimate understanding that much more is to come in Heaven. Thank You.

Fishing Tip: How to keep from losing your fresh salmon-egg bait in a strong current: Sprinkle the eggs lightly with table salt and go fishing immediately. The "rubberized" eggs will then stay on your hook.

> *For if ye forgive men their trespasses, your heavenly Father will also forgive you.*
> —Matthew 6:14

FORGIVENESS

For several years I was editor of a small fishing magazine called *The Keystone Sportsman*. I was also the reporter, photographer, layout designer, printer, and janitor. That was just in my spare time. Full time, I was a homicide detective for the Tulsa, Oklahoma, police department, with a second part-time position as Director of Criminal Justice, American Christian College. On the cover of one issue of *The Sportsman*, I used what has to be my favorite photo of my son Michael. He was four-years-old and stood on a pond bank proudly displaying a string of fat perch. The fly of his little jeans gaped open while he attempted to hold up his pants with his free hand.

The photo represents treasured memories of going fishing with my sons, as Paw had fished with me. Every time I had a rare day off from work, I collected the boys and we headed for the nearest body of water with a full minnow bucket and a stash of fishing worms. I wanted to share with them my love and appreciation of nature and the outdoors, instill in them that sense of tranquility that comes from water, skies, and open country.

Dianne divorced me when Michael was nine, David eleven. Joshua, whom I adopted, hadn't come along yet. Not that divorce was a surprise, although I was devastated nonetheless.

By that time, I had been a cop for about fourteen years—four in Miami, Florida, where I met and married Dianne, and nearly ten in Tulsa. I had always tried to protect my family from my life on the mean streets of the city. I even bought a small ranch in the country an hour away from Tulsa. What I failed to protect them from was the disillusion that sooner or later infected the soul of every cop. Being a cop embitters a man, destroys all illusions about any natural goodness that may or may not be inherent in humanity. Dianne could never seem to understand why I was no longer the happy-go-lucky man she wed. I sometimes caught her staring at me, as though offended by the tough street cop I had become.

She was utterly appalled when I killed a man in a gunfight. "You mean you can kill somebody and you're so hardened that it doesn't even bother you?" she cried.

"Had you rather it be him—or me?" I responded.

After that, it bothered me because it *didn't* bother me. That I could take a life and not be touched by it, however justified it may have been. Although I wasn't yet a Christian, I couldn't help but consider God's Commandment: *Thou Shall Not Kill.*

Dianne grew more and more aloof. Then she took our sons back to Florida, where I was no longer essential to their daily lives, leaving me alone with my anger and resentment. I became a long-distance dad who would no longer go fishing with my sons—or much of anything else, for that matter. A superfluous father.

Dianne remarried in Florida. My two sons graduated from school and went on to college. Through various subtle means and from motives I still don't quite understand, my ex-wife successfully estranged me from my children. A heavy smoker, she contracted lung cancer in her early forties. She ended up in a hostel within a short period of time, her condition terminal. She telephoned me a few weeks before she died.

"I want to make things right," she said. "I was wrong to divorce you, and I was wrong to take away your sons. You were a good father and a good husband. Chuck, I'm begging for your forgiveness before I die."

Tears filled my eyes. She began crying over the phone. I was no Christian yet. God and I had been warring all my life as I struggled, without His help—or so I thought—to comprehend the Vast Unknown of time and space and life. I hadn't known it, but all along I was somehow absorbing lessons taught by

Jesus nearly two millennium previously.

Jesus preached forgiveness. *"...Forgive, and ye shall be forgiven."* (Luke 6:37)

To forgive was required as part of living the good life.

I cried with and for my ex-wife. That was the last time I spoke to her. She died not long afterward. Michael was a grown young man by then and no longer the little boy holding up his pants on the bank of a pond. We went fishing together again off a secret little island we knew in the Florida Keys. Dianne had tried to make things right before she died.

Lord, make my heart as vast as the seas so that I may always forgive others.

Fishing Tip: Graphite rods are conductors of electricity and may be dangerous in a lightning storm. If the sky looks nasty, put down your rods and get off the water.

> *The testimony of the Lord is sure, and giveth wisdom unto the simple.*
> —Psalm 19:7

SIMPLICITY

Having grown up in the foothills of the Ozark Mountains, I like to think of myself today as having been more than a ragged, dirty little kid with a cane fishing pole. Not that there is anything wrong with being a simple hillbilly kid. I was happy roaming the mountains with a few hounds, hunting the woods and fishing the streams, roasting squirrels and perch over an open fire. The Bible speaks often of the good and simple life. Kipling suggested that we be taught "delight in simple things."

Even back then I dreamed of becoming a writer.

In 1979, I resigned from the Tulsa Police Department where I was a homicide detective in order to live my dream of becoming a fulltime freelance writer. As a cop, I had witnessed crime, violence and evil for the past fourteen years. It was my contention that the misery we suffer on this planet is largely due to the human heart gone bad. I sometimes thought God might have made a mistake in creating mankind. In His place, perhaps, I would have made platypuses, octopi, elephants and bass, but never Adam and Eve. Civilization had lost all meaning for me. I needed to get as far away from it as possible.

I purchased five acres of scrub woodland so far back in the mountains of eastern Oklahoma that even deer needed topographical maps to find their way around. On a single afternoon in early spring, I built what became known as "The Tool Shed," an 8x16-foot plywood building with a tin roof, one door, and a single Plexiglas window. I painted the front and one side green, ran out of paint and finished it in melon. Inside was room enough for a bed at one end and a desk and book shelves at the other. No electricity, no telephone ringing, the only plumbing a one-holer outhouse I erected nearby.

It was the era of the "get back to earth" movement. *Mother Earth News, Farmstead* Magazine, the *Foxfire* books. Fed up with civilization and all its baggage, people like me were eager to search for real meaning in the soil, simplify our lives, get back to basics and start all over again. It didn't seem much of a hardship to me since I had grown up not so much differently, so poor even poverty was a step up.

The surrounding woodlands were full of squirrels, rabbits and deer, and the Illinois River ran past within walking distance and emptied into the Arkansas River. A man who had grown up hunting and fishing and harvesting wild poke weed, nuts and berries would never starve. I also intended to truck crop, grow a few chickens and keep a goat for milking. My Creek Indian ancestors (I'm a quarter-breed) had lived okay.

I felt rich in my new simplicity.

My first wife Dianne had left me the year before. I was now engaged to marry Kathy, a beautiful young blond with a one year-old son, Joshua, from a previous marriage. I took her out to "The Farm."

"I can make it as a writer," I assured her. "You can come with me or not. It's your choice and I want you to know it's your choice. Either way, I have to give writing a chance."

We married and moved into The Tool Shed. Kathy, Joshua, me, a St. Bernard dog named Hildegard, and a baby goat named Izzy. Very quickly we settled into a routine. Early each morning I rose to write at my desk by kerosene lamp, exactly the way I had as a kid. The rest of the day I cleared plots for truck gardens, built a chicken house, and started construction on our *real* house.

Money was tight, but I managed to sell enough articles and short stories to provide our staples. My first novel, *No Gentle Streets*, was published to critical acclaim, but sold only modestly. Eventually, we grew vegetables, corn and melons, and lived off the land: pokeweed and wild onions with scrambled homegrown eggs, wild blackberry cobbler, pecans, black walnuts, mushrooms, fried rabbit, squirrels, ducks, venison, and lots of fish from the rivers. Trout and channel cat, bream and largemouth bass, carp and buffalo, gar I shot with a bow and arrow.

Even though we lived simply, we went without none of life's essentials. We grew brown and strong from living and working in the outdoors. Joshua and I often canoed the Illinois River, catching trout for dinner. I sometimes thought of how Jesus took the loaf of bread and two fishes and provided for the multitudes.

Those were joyful days without television or the outside world. We regained touch with life's simple pleasures. Watching together a sunset or a moonrise. Enjoying an afternoon fishing in the summer sun. Swimming in the river. After nightfall, after Kathy had cooked dinner on a Coleman camp stove, we built a fire in front of The Tool Shed and sat around it content in conversation and each other's company. Friends came by sometimes to help rekindle the lost art of storytelling. Hildegard and Izzy Goat stretched out together by the fire. Wobbles our pet Mallard duck strutted over and squatted next to the pallet on which Joshua had finally fallen asleep. Times of true value.

We lived in The Tool Shed for eight months before I completed construction of the *real* house. Eventually, I became successful enough as a writer that we no longer *had* to eat pokeweed and fish every day. However, some of the happiest days of our lives were lived fully in the little green-and-melon Tool Shed. Henry David Thoreau had lived similarly more than a century earlier, as he recounted in *Walden*. Jesus owned little more than the robe he wore, his sandals, a crown of thorns at the end and... faith that love, wisdom and understanding flourished in the simple life.

Dear Heavenly Father, let us understand that all the wealth accumulated in this world is nothing but dead leaves and stagnant water, for it is in the simple life of faith that we store riches in Your world.

Fishing Tip: "Dead sticking" plastic worms—letting them settle on the bottom for twenty to 45 seconds—is often most successful in reservoirs or lakes with very clear water, especially when there is a slight bottom current to make the worm's ribbon tail move back and forth.

Which doeth great things past finding out;
yea, and wonders without numbers.
—Job 9:10

WONDER

My fishing buddy D and I had a favorite catfishing spot on a small creek that could only be reached by canoe or on foot. We would put the canoe in at an access point and paddle upstream, jigging around deadfalls and brush for crappie. After nightfall, we beached the canoe on a sandbar and still-fished a deep, narrow cut for channel cat, using blood bait or live worms.

Cottonwood, sweet gum and willows arched over the creek, forming a dark tunnel into which no moon or starlight penetrated. After midnight or so, we paddled back out through the tunnel until, reaching a certain bend, we suddenly emerged into full moonshine. The experience never failed to fill me with a deep sense of wonder and mystery. What mortal could witness it and not believe in God? As Thomas Carlyle wrote back in the 19th Century, "worship is transcendent wonder."

"But be ye glad and rejoice for ever in that which I create." (Isaiah 65:18)

The moon, especially during its full phase, shined directly down the middle of the stream, making it seem that we glided along on a highway of silver liquid. From above, stars laughed so bright and dense down through a gap between the trees that it seemed I could lift my arms and fly among them.

One night, I spotted a beaver trailing starlight across the creek. I always believed God had a sense of humor. Drawing D's attention to the glory of the heavens, I silently drove the canoe toward the beaver. D sat in the prow while I paddled. I slapped the creek with my paddle when I drew near, whereupon the startled creature slapped back, splashing D with water.

I have spent many wonderful nights like that on creek or river banks—while backpacking, canoeing, or in the bush with Army Special Forces. Contemplating the mysteries of God's creations, mysteries hidden and deep, attempting with all my cerebral might to fathom what might be *out there*. If I do make it to heaven, the first thing I intend to request is: God, I want to know *everything*. Will you please tell me now?

In the meantime, we who are mortal and Earthbound shall never unravel the enigmas of infinity and eternity. Although we are surrounded by miracles, we fail to understand or even to see most of them. Out blindness to them reminds me of a record-breaking transcontinental flight I made in an ultralite aircraft called a powered parachute.

A PPC (powered parachute) resembled a dandelion seed, a go cart-like affair suspended beneath a square parachute that serves as a wing. Since its top airspeed is about thirty mph, it took me 23 days to fly from San Diego, California, to St. Mary's, Georgia.

While flying at an altitude of about 1,000 feet over Mobile Bay in Alabama, I looked down upon two men in a boat fishing on calm waters. In the water off to one side lurked a monster shark longer than their boat. I could see it clearly from my vantage point high above. From theirs, it was invisible.

Theirs was the perfect metaphor for man on Earth. Wonder and mystery are all around us, few of which we ever even notice. We live in two worlds, both equally wondrous. One world we see, one we do not. There is always more going on than meets the eye.

Lord, give me eyes to see, the mind to comprehend, and the heart to encompass the magnitude of Your universe and rejoice in its wonders.

Fishing Tip: Microplugs for trout are not strictly river tackle. They're also useful in trout lakes for fish prowling inshore shallows or weed beds.

Create in me a clean heart, O God; and renew a right spirit within me...
—Psalm 51:10

REJUVENATE

Miami, Florida, was once a swamp that must be constantly drained to prevent the city from sinking back into the bog. Drainage canals snake out of the city and its suburbs and empty into the Atlantic Ocean. One of these man-made canals runs through North Miami where I lived with my wife Dianne while I was a City of Miami police officer. Next to the canal, amidst the urban sprawl, grew a lone palm in a vacant lot.

As a cop, I worked black ghettos with the highest crime rates in the nation. Violence and social rot prevailed. I was cursed, called "pig," shot at, assaulted with clubs, rocks, knives, teeth and claws. People inflicted horrible atrocities upon each other. I saw babies beaten with clothes hangers and boiled alive in hot water. Theft, arson, assault, robbery, and murder was a way of life.

Although I liked the excitement and adventure of attempting to bring law and order to a lawless society, being a cop could cause one to lose his perspective and abandon his faith in mankind and, if he weren't careful, in God. I was still a country boy at heart who sometimes longed for mountains and wild streams and the nearest neighbor a mile away. The lone palm tree in the vacant lot surrounded by the bustle and clamor of a modern city was my refuge. At every opportunity, I grabbed a fishing rod and daydreamed away an afternoon with my back against the palm while I caught a few grunt or yellowtail.

I always left my oasis feeling rejuvenated and ready to take on crime once again. I figured God must have provided the palm to save my soul from encasing itself in a shell impenetrable to love, compassion, and, ultimately, to Him.

I realize all these years later, Lord, that You are my palm tree, my refuge, that You rejuvenate my soul.

> **Fishing Tip:** For shore anglers below dams and along the banks of big reservoirs, the ability to cast long distances is a prerequisite to catching more and bigger fish.

A friend loveth at all times.
—Proverbs 17:17

FRIENDSHIP

Alone, the library of the two-story house my wife Donna Sue (fourth wife, and last) built on our GG Ranch in Oklahoma is three times the size of The Tool Shed Kathy, Joshua and I lived in when I resigned from the Tulsa Police Department to become a fulltime freelance writer. Grandchildren and friends refer to the library as "The Museum." Displayed in it are mementos and souvenirs from many years of travel and adventure: the jaw of the piranha that bit me on the Amazon River; an Arab's robe given to me in Algeria; shark's teeth from the Gulf of Mexico; a wad of camel hair from Egypt; a coin from Sir Frances Drake's treasure; a South American blowgun; a sled dog harness; my paratrooper helmet, boots and Green Beret uniform; the rib bone of a whale; a sea lion's skull; Anasazi pottery...

On one wall between a mounted flying pheasant and the tail feathers of a grouse, above a black bear skin rug, hangs a largemouth bass of eight pounds or so. I look at it and I see a summer's day years ago, a five-acre pond, and big Bill McCracken. Bill was my partner on the police Homicide Detail and my friend for over thirty years. The last thing he said to me before he died was, "I love you, Bro'."

"Will'm, you are my brother."

Death is a fact of life, especially significant as we grow older. Bill and I always went fishing together.

"A man that hath friends must shew himself friendly; and there is a friend that sticketh closer than a brother." (Proverbs 18:24)

Only Jesus could have been closer.

It is sometimes observed that fortunate indeed is the man who can go through life and claim one true friend. For a man hardened as I have been by wars and crime fighting, I am more fortunate than most people to claim several friends of that designation. Bill, I think, was a gift from God. I learned to depend on him. He never let me down.

McCracken had been in Homicide three or four years while I was still working the streets as a member of a special police SWAT/TAC squad. He was assigned the investigation after I was involved in a shootout one night. He introduced himself by calling me on the telephone the morning after my shift ended.

"When you get time," he said, "I need to take a statement. Get some sleep first."

A year later I earned a detective's shield and was assigned to Homicide. The division sergeant put me with McCracken for my breaking-in period. I strode self-consciously into the big detectives' bullpen, trying to appear nonchalant in the cheap baggy suit purchased with my new clothing allowance.

McCracken swung his booted feet off his desk top. He was a big man with a prominent scar across his upper lip.

"Welcome to the Cuckoo's Nest," he greeted in his laconic manner. "We'll have another case soon. People *enjoy* killing each other."

It was a tough squad. Fully half the men on the shift had killed other men in gunfights. Jack Powell shot and killed a doper; Harold Harrison shot a burglar; Doc Roberts once killed a car thief; for McCracken it was a bang-away gunfight with an armed robber; and for me...it was *Moses*.

Before Tulsa, I had been a cop in Miami, Florida. The ghetto riots that accompanied the 1968 Republican National Convention on Miami Beach had been going on for three days before I shot Moses in a firefight. I shot him through the lungs. I killed a man named *Moses*.

I ended up in the hospital later that night. An FBI friend delivered me home on crutches. My white uniform shirt was crusted with blood. My wife Dianne stared aghast at the blood and whiskers and grime and my torn uniform. It was the first time she actually realized what kind of occupation I had chosen.

Wives, it seemed, came and went. Only another cop could understand the mean streets and what it did to us. We seldom had to justify ourselves to each other. But Bill McCracken was always there whenever I needed him, no matter what.

One afternoon, I found myself alone in a house full of thieves, dopers, and a murder suspect who had tortured and electrocuted an elderly woman during a home breaking. I needed to make arrests, but there were guns everywhere and I knew any attempt to arrest would likely end in a shootout. I was outnumbered by six to one. I managed to signal McCracken. A few minutes later, the big ex-Marine kicked the front door off its hinges and burst in with a shotgun at the ready to take on all the demons in hell. I grinned around at the assemblage.

"You're all under arrest," I announced. "First one tries anything gets a load of buckshot."

I remember that day—and many others like it. But my best memories are reserved for fishing with Bill. We would lie on a creek bank together or kick back in our boat and hold long philosophical conversations about the meaning and purpose of things. A cop can lose his perspective on life if he isn't careful. We often spoke of God, pondering, wondering why, if He *really* existed, He allowed evil to exist in our world. With Bill, while fishing, I took small steps toward an eventual closer understanding of God's purpose.

I smile whenever I look at the big mounted bass on my wall. It reminds me of Bill, of friendship, and of the long journey I made to reach God.

I pray that I am blessed to live a life that deserves friends willing to give everything for friendship, that I can give in return, and that I embrace Jesus as the Best Friend of all.

Fishing Tip: Sweeten your small perch spoons with maggot for more action.

A time to love and a time to hate; a time of war, and a time of peace.
—Ecclesiastes 3:8

PEACE

Whenever as a homicide cop I felt my skin growing thin and the case load heavy, I sought peace by escaping to a place I knew on remote Haskell Lake. It was a small lake, perhaps twenty acres, girded by low banks of rock and jumbled boulders with a flat shallows at one end overgrown with saw grass, cattails, and lily pads. My oldest son David was reaching an age when he liked to fish.

The only access to the lake was a potholed dirt road, which meant we rarely saw anyone there. David and I fished the lily pads for largemouth and bluegill. After nightfall, we fried fish over an open fire. Generally, we had pan-fried potatoes, too, and a can of pork 'n beans washed down by Pepsi kept cool in the lake.

Later, in our sleeping bags, David sometimes felt talkative.

"Daddy? What's that, Daddy?"

"An owl, Big Dave."

"Daddy, it's *dark.*"

"It's always this dark at night, Dave. Look up through the trees at the stars."

"Daddy, do other people live on the stars?"

"I wouldn't be surprised if they did. What do you think?"

"Are they... Do you think they're *monsters,* Daddy?"

"Monsters live only in peoples' minds, son."

"If people live on the stars, what do they look like?"

"Maybe they have one leg or a dozen eyes or something."

"Daddy, can we get up real early in the morning and fish before we go home?"

"That's why we come to the lake."

"Daddy, 'member that big bass I caught up here last time? I

caught him all by myself."

"You sure did. He was bigger than mine."

"Daddy, how come nobody but us comes here to fish?"

"Maybe not many people know about it."

"Maybe they're scared of *ghosts.*"

"I think mostly they're scared of being alone."

"Were you ever lonesome, Daddy?"

"Sometimes."

"Was that before you met Mommy?"

"Mostly."

"Does Mommy like you, Daddy?"

"I hope so."

"Do you like her?"

"She's your mother, son. I married her."

"Does that mean you like her?"

"Yes."

"I heard you and Mommy talking. She said you wasn't happy 'cause you can't be married to the police and her too. Daddy, I don't ever want to be married. If I become a policeman too, can policemen live with their mommies and daddies?"

"You can live with us as long as you want."

"Daddy, did you ever shoot anybody?"

"Yes."

"Did he shoot you too?"

"Are you warm enough, Dave?"

"Can we come and sleep on the ground again?"

"I promise. We'll camp out lots of times."

"Daddy, do you know something? Good things happen, don't they?"

He went to sleep. I watched his sleeping face in the moonlight. Then I got up and made my way to the low bluff by the lake and sat there watching the water gentle in the night. It was warm out, but I shivered anyhow. I often had trouble sleeping, my mind poisoned by cop's thoughts of death and violence. I tried to fight them off, but it was like being mugged.

In my mind's eye, I saw the wads of maggots in murder victim Suzanne Oakley's ears. I saw the mouse darting from the mouth of the bloated corpse in the basement. I saw more maggots glued like softballs to the heads of people who had blown out their brains. I smelled death rot from the morgue. A horror video of grisly, mutilated faces and bodies. I sometimes joked about death being contagious. Sooner or later it caught up to all of us.

"You can talk to me," Dianne promised. "I want you to share things with me."

"All I see is dying and violence," I said, trying. "It makes me think every day that I'm dying too."

Horror flooded her eyes. She didn't want to share *these* things.

Sitting in the moonlight by the lake, I felt the presence of a kind of terror growing inside. I had nightmares when I was asleep, but now I was awake and having them. It felt like the skin was rotting off my bones. I had to look to make sure it wasn't. I felt alone and small and mostly alone because a cop was always alone in vital parts of himself and couldn't touch and be touched and still be a cop. A cop was always at war with crime and evil.

Like Teddy Roosevelt said, "It is only the warlike power of a civilized people that can give peace to the world."

I grasped my legs and pulled my knees up to my chin and dropped my head onto my arms. And then, alone, I cried for a very long time and never ever told anyone about it. Not even God.

God is still teaching me about peace. The nearest I come to it is when I am alone with God in nature.

Lord, I know that I will find true peace only in You.

Fishing Tip: Subtle variations in bait and presentation often means the difference between a full creel and an empty one. Observe baitfish in the area and approximate their color, size and movements.

> *For every one that asketh receiveth; and he that seeketh findeth; and to him that knocketh it shall be opened.*
> —Matthew 7:8

UNDERSTANDING

I love stories of transformation and understanding. Cinderella or the Phoenix rising from their cinders or ashes. The Ugly Duckling turning into a beautiful swan, the frog into a prince, or Pinocchio into a real boy. The Cowardly Lion obtains courage, the Scarecrow gets brains, and the Tin Man wins a new heart. All transformed through greater understanding or courage into that which they longed to be but never thought they would be.

Transformation and understanding are essential ingredients of any great story. They are the secret to Christianity, and Christianity is the secret to the universe. My personal road to discovering that secret was long and ragged and had many twists and turns. The Mississippi River was a leg of that journey after my first wife Dianne divorced me. I was bitter and angry at her, disgusted and discouraged with life.

"Wisdom is the principal thing;" Proverbs 4:7 reminds us. *"Therefore get wisdom; and with all thy getting get understand."*

From the time my sons David and Michael started walking, I had taken them flying (I'm a pilot), rubber boating, SCUBA diving, horseback riding, motorcycling... Adventure to a boy is as necessary as water to a desert sourdough. Life, I stressed, is to be lived with vigor.

Dianne left me in March and raced back to Florida where we had met and married, taking my sons with her. The boys returned to spend the summer with me. David was eleven, Michael nine. They had been reading *Huckleberry Finn*.

"Let's float on a raft," they suggested.

Together, with ten-year-old David McCracken, the son of my police partner Bill, we constructed a raft with a plywood deck eight feet wide and ten feet long mounted on three thick Styrofoam pontoons. An old army poncho served as a cabin. The boys promptly christened the raft *Huck Finn*.

"You're floating the Mississippi River on that!" friends exclaimed.

The Huck Finn way, floating the currents without power other than oars, taking our leisure to fish, skinny dip, sunbathe, and explore mysterious island for river pirate treasure.

Three excited boys and I shoved off into darkly-running waters beneath the Greenville Bridge near Port Pleasant, Arkansas. The raft bobbed like a cork. It raced beneath the bridge in the current and thrust into the wider river beyond.

For the next weeks, we rafters discovered the mysteries, the beauty, and, yes, the capriciousness of the mighty Father of Waters. In places, the river yawned out to a mile wide where the flow was gentle and slow. The crew aboard the raft played games, napped in the sun, swam or fished off the stern, exchanged greetings with passing fishermen displaying catfish and drum half as large as a man, and avoided tugs each pushing its charge of twenty to thirty loaded barges.

In other places, the river deepened and narrowed and went crashing between high muddy walls and skidding around sandbars and over man-made jetties designed to control and direct the power of the continent's excess water on its way to the sea. Tricky currents swept raft and riders over hidden snags or banged them against jetties and submerged rocks. The river determined our progress. Some days we struggled to log five miles. Others, we easily floated thirty. *Huck Finn* sometimes creaked and protested under the rigors of the journey, but it held fast.

Dining was on simple fare easily carried and stored, such as canned goods, cereal, and potatoes. We moored each afternoon in time to catch channel cat for dinner, fried in grease in an iron skillet over an open fire. I taught the boys how to bake potatoes and bread wrapped in tinfoil and buried in beds of hot coals.

The movement of the water, the warm sun, leisurely days and nights of gentle companionship with my sons and their friend, fishing from the raft or from the banks of the river gradually washed some of the anger and bitterness from my soul. A little inner voice assured me that great and wonderful things were yet in store for me—if I continued to seek understanding not only of myself but also of a Creator who had provided all these wonders for mankind's delight. Although still a doubter, a questioner, I looked up at the stars and vowed to work spiritually to reform myself into a person more worthy of love and trust.

"Thank You," I murmured. "Whoever You might be."

Father, I ask that You continue to open the doors to understanding for the rest of my life on earth, and that I develop with Your help the wisdom to transform from an Ugly Duckling of sin to a swan in Your eyes.

> **Fishing Tip:** Warming water temperatures as the ice recedes in the Great Lakes trigger a salmon feeding spree each spring along the coasts.

And all things, whatsoever you shall ask in prayer, believing, ye shall receive.
   —Matthew 21:22

PRAYER

I took Donna Sue squirrel hunting on our first date. I'm a romantic devil, if nothing else. Then I took her fly fishing for trout in New Mexico. There she was—blond, all five-one of her looking like a tiny waif unexpectedly dropped into rubber waders far too big for her. She plunged through cattails and reeds towering above her head and, undaunted by the swift water, whipped her fly rod right alongside mine.

My kind of lady.

I can't gloss it over. I had been married three times by the time I met Donna Sue in 1995. I was also a confirmed bachelor by then, having been single for some ten years with the exception of a brief wartime interlude with Nita after I volunteered for *Desert Storm*, the first Iraqi war. Life with me can be difficult for a woman, what with my gallivanting off all over the world chasing stories or going to wars.

Comparing notes, Donna Sue and I concluded we had actually met as far back as 1973 when I was editor of *The Keystone Sportsman* magazine and she owned and operated a bait shop on Keystone Lake. Each month I personally distributed copies of the publication to all the businesses who advertised with me, including Donna Sue's. The businesses then passed out the magazines to their customers. Neither of us was to remember the other those years later when we became reacquainted. I had been married to Dianne back then, Donna Sue was married to Dean Cagle, who drowned while fishing in the lake.

"I think I should warn you," she said. "My first two husbands died."

Her second husband, Olan, died of cancer.

"That's okay," I said. "I've got enough luck for the both of us. I've been stabbed once and shot once in the head and I'm still alive."

I was cynical and cautious at first. What can you bring to another if your heart is empty, dried up, pinned down? However, for the first time in my life, with Donna Sue, I *felt* truly loved, unconditionally loved. So far, we've been married twelve years, a new record for me. She is the best, the most perfect human being I've ever known. She taught me love—and God through her and her son Darren, taught me the value of prayer.

"I was so fortunate to find Chuck," Donna Sue said.

"Luck had nothing to do with it," Darren said. "I prayed and asked God for him."

Being an unsaved heathen, I wasn't much for prayer in those days. But, still, there was something I never told Donna Sue: I had also prayed in my own single-thought manner that I would meet someone I could keep and who would keep me, warts and all.

"One single grateful thought raised to heaven is the most perfect prayer," Minna von Barnhelm wrote in the Eighteenth Century.

God answered Darren's prayer—and mine.

A simple prayer, Lord: Thank You. For all things.

Fishing Tip: To kill parasites in fish before eating: cook at 145 degrees Fahrenheit until the fish flakes; or freeze fish at -4 degrees for seven days.

> *"Verily I say unto you, Whatever ye shall bind on earth shall be bound in heaven..."*
> —Matthew 18:18

HEAVEN

Whenever I was growing up, my family never attended church except when some itinerant preacher traveling through the mountains stopped to hold revival in a country church or an abandoned one-room schoolhouse. Every night for a week there would be singing and shouting, rolling on the floor and speaking in tongues. Ol' Earnest Waters would run around outside chasing Jesus and yelling, "Catch him! Catch him!"

Revivals scared me to death. I lived with the nagging fear that God was going to get me. Revivals were never about bringing the love of God to mankind; they were intended to scare Hell out of us. There was always talk about Hell and Hell fire and how sinners were going to be cast into the fiery pit to burn for eternity and more eternity.

Heaven was scarcely mentioned except in passing. "Do you want to go to Heaven, or do you want to burn in Hell?" Heaven was vaguely described as a place of mansions and streets of gold where angels sang twenty four hours a day. I wondered if that was all there was to it. I didn't want to go to Hell, but Heaven didn't seem all that enticing either.

If I learned about a revival soon enough to avoid it, I grabbed my cane fishing pole and a can of worms and sneaked off running as hard as I could across the meadow to the creek. Mom would shout for me a time or two, which I ignored, before she shook her head in exasperation and latched onto my brothers Joe and Kenneth before they also had a chance to disappear.

My escaping couldn't be all *that* bad. After all, wasn't I following God's commandments?

"Go thou to the seas, and cast a hook, and take up the fish

that first cometh up..." (Matthew 17:27)

"Behold, I will send for many fishers, saith the Lord..." (Jeremiah 16:16)

"Simon Peter saith unto him, I go a fishing..." (John 21:3)

Well, I go a fishing too.

Carp infested many of the streams of eastern Oklahoma. While modern sports fishermen consider the carp a bone-infested trash fish and refuse to eat them, we in the hills during those lean years ate a lot of them. 'Possums too. Carp were big and thick with lots of meat. They were easy to catch using worms or dough balls for bait. They were also tough, scrappy fish who put up a good fight.

One revival evening, having gone on the lam, I was sitting barefoot on the creek bank daydreaming when a yank nearly pulled the pole from my hands. I leaped to my feet and yanked back. The pole fractured into two pieces. I cast aside my end and grabbed for what remained.

That piece also broke as the monster on the other end of the line threw its weight against me. I slipped on the muddy bank and fell, clawing frantically at the last short section of cane skittering down the bank toward the creek. It speared unhesitatingly into the water and went bobbing merrily downstream.

I sat down and began to laugh softly as I watched the remnants of my fishing pole being towed around a bend in the creek. What a great fish. I felt totally content simply sitting there by the creek while I enjoyed the sunset through the cottonwoods. It occurred to me then and at other times that maybe the preachers were wrong about Heaven. God would never take a half-wild little kid like me and expect me to be happy on streets of gold or rattling around in a mansion. Lord, just a cabin in the woods on a creek bank would do nicely.

God, did You not say that You would create "new heavens and a new earth?" (Isaiah 65:17). And, Lord, did You not also admonish us to "be ye glad and rejoice for ever in that which I create?" (Isaiah 65:18)

> **Fishing Tip:** In ice fishing, focus on location: points extending from shore into the deepest parts of the lake; isolated structure within the main basin of the lake, such as reefs and sunken islands; sharp drops or breaks separating structure from deep water.

Every man shall give as he is able, according to the blessing of the Lord thy God which he hath given thee.
—Deuteronomy 16:17

GENEROSITY

"It is therefore our business," wrote the philosopher Edmund Burke, "to cultivate in our minds, to rear to the most perfect vigor and maturity, every sort of generous and honest feeling that belongs to our nature."

I have a tendency to be selfish at times. God, I think, chose the "Thanksgiving Day Shark" to teach me a lesson in the habit of generosity.

By virtue of its geographical detachment from the rest of the United States, Key West, Florida, has always been something of a "last resort" for various colorful flotsam and jetsam washed upon tropical shores. The Conch Train stopped at Cow Key Channel to allow tourists in baggy drawers and funny hats the opportunity to snapshot what was once commonly referred to as "The Anchorage."

As a freelance writer and novelist making my name, I found the island's romance and allure irresistible. That was where I lived—at The Anchorage on a seventeen-foot Newport sailboat dubbed *Gandalf.* After all, Key West had been the home of the Great Guru Ernest Hemingway.

Although I frequently set sail for adventure and parts unknown around the rim of the Caribbean, there was no experience quite like returning to The Anchorage under reduced sail at sunset. The air itself seemed to turn a little, well, *wacky*. Few ports in the sailing world offered a body politic so *diverse. Downright loony* might be a better description.

As in conventional communities ashore, The Anchorage was composed of two distinct and non-interactive neighborhoods. Along Roosevelt Boulevard stretched "Houseboat Row," snobbish, sniffish, old blue blood elite. Some of the houseboats were valued at a quarter-mil or so and were so permanently attached to the seawall that barnacles anchored them in place.

The riffraff, the rabble, the *hoi poi*, the unwashed lived out in the channel anchored in old tin houseboats, motor cruisers without motors, dilapidated sailboats—the most extraordinary collection of vessels ever assembled in one place. With "live-aboarders" to match.

Each evening just before dusk, a twelve-string guitar began strumming background music from the shuttered-off recesses of an old cabin cruiser isolated over near the mangroves. The music was haunting and blue—the wailing of a jilted lover, a disillusioned vagabond, a rolling stone finally stopped to gather moss. Live-aboarders paused to listen and discreetly wipe tears.

The boat never moved except to float one direction or another on its anchor with the exchange of tides between the Gulf and the Atlantic. I never laid eyes on the guitar maestro, not once. I called him "The Ghost."

On the other hand, the Dykes on Bikes were highly visible, having apparently been sumo wrestlers in previous lifetimes. The list of their old tin-and-sheet metal houseboat announced whenever both moved to either port or starboard at the same time. Sometimes they got drunk in Jimmy Buffet's downtown "Margaritaville" and belligerently ensconced themselves on the little dinghy dock where residents moored their rubber boats, pint-sized dinghies, or surfboards when they went ashore. Like a pair of Little Johns in Sherwood Forest, they indiscriminately challenged the right of one and sundry to pass. Failure to pay the toll of one beer—even hesitation in paying it—subjected the cheapskate to a prompt dunking.

A little fellow called "Superman," who lived aboard his sloop with fourteen or so cats, got very, very drunk and made a regrettable pass at one of the Dykes and promptly suffered the consequences of being stabbed with a knife by the other. Not seriously as it turned out.

That was the only act of unbridled passion I ever witnessed at The Anchorage. For the most part, the denizens of the shallows were a peaceable and fun-loving sort.

The relationship between George and Wanda was a mysterious thing. They owned one of the better boats at Cow Key Channel. Wanda had muscular dystrophy, necessitating that George tote her around like an infant, transferring her tenderly from boat to dinghy to shore or another boat.

Wanda developed a crush on me. In the middle of a night, especially following a communal fish fry on one or another of the boats, her plaintive cry shrieked across the still water like that of a human sea gull: "Chuckie! Chuckie, will you come sleep with me?"

By far the most colorful inhabitant of The Anchorage had to be Bill Bailey. Maybe it was his true name, perhaps not, for live-aboarders came and went with privacy and anonymity. One house boater called himself Albert Q. Einstein.

Bill and his girlfriend Jeannie lived on a ratty houseboat that even a modest trade wind threatened to swamp. Their head (toilet) consisted of a five-gallon paint bucket and a roll of toilet paper. Their dinghy was a surfboard. Social types, Bill and his white cat Scavenger scooted about the channel on their board, the cat splay-footed in front, Bill on his knees paddling wild-haired and wild-bearded and often all but naked.

Each time Bill and Jeannie quarreled, which was often and often late at night, Bill and Scavenger took off together on the surfboard and left Jeannie singing her little heart out across the dark waters:

> *"Oh, won't you come home, Bill Bailey...?*
> *"Oh, won't you come home..."*
> *"I know I've done you wrong..."*

Fish were abundant in schools around old wrecks sunk in the channel. I caught snapper and grunt and an occasional yellowfin or small grouper. Just before Thanksgiving, Bill

Bailey landed a nurse shark about five feet long. Such a bounty was excuse enough to gather the clans for a community fish fry and beer bust that resembled the bar scenes from *Star Wars*. These were poor folks, but each brought to the Thanksgiving feast whatever he had to offer or could afford, an outpouring of generosity that touched me deeply. Just before Bill carved the "Thanksgiving Shark," someone suggested we give thanks.

Heads bowed in unison inside the single room of Bill's old houseboat. One of the *Star Wars* cast began to recite a prayer with genuine feeling: "Lord, thank You for Your generosity on this Thanksgiving Day and for the blessings we are about to receive..."

Lord, thank You every day for the bounties of life—and help guide me to cultivate in my mind generosity and a generous feeling toward all.

Fishing Tip: Some of the most prolific shark fishing in the United States may be experienced in the deep cuts dividing the string of islands of the Florida Keys. Fish for them as you would for fresh water catfish, using a tight line and other fish for bait.

> *"I beseech you therefore, brethren, by the mercies of God, that ye present your bodies in living sacrifice, holy, acceptable unto God, which is your reasonable service."*
> —Romans 12:1

SACRIFICE

During the Siege of Britain in 1940, a young RAF pilot named V.A. Rosewarne died in action over the English Channel. His last letter to his mother ended with, "The universe is so vast and ageless that the life of one man can only be justified by the measure of his sacrifice."

Jesus' death on the cross to atone for human sins is the greatest sacrifice ever made. It continues to inspire all of us, even though we may be unaware of it. I believe my son David and I were destined to be at a particular point at a particular time to serve God, to be used for good even at the chance of sacrificing ourselves.

David had graduated from Duke University Medical School. That summer, he and I took off to backpack, hike and occasionally fish all over the American West. The Grand Canyon, Yellowstone Park, Grand Tetons, the Rockies... In Utah, we backpacked rugged Mt. Zion National Forest for a few days, then relaxed with a leisurely hike up the Virgin River. So many of the lessons God has taught me involves wildernesses and fishing streams.

The trail along the Virgin is a popular tourist attraction cut into the side of the sheer rock canyon that encloses the stream. The cliffs are literally unscaleable without proper rock climbing equipment, which means the only way in and out is via the trail back to the Ranger Station.

The trail dead ends about three miles up the river. It was an incredible day, warm, sun shining. David and I waded upstream another mile or so. Sheer rock cliffs hundreds of feet in height walled in the stream. At some points you could touch either wall while standing in the middle of the river. Trout darted through the water like slivers of reflected light.

Flash floods are always a threat in high desert country. Thunder rumbling off in the distance persuaded us to return to the trailhead.

By the time we splashed back downstream, ominous black clouds had corked up the canyon and a cold deluge of rain howled down upon us, causing instant mudslides and waterfalls from the cliffs above. Temperatures that had been near the 80s suddenly plummeted. At trail's end, about sixteen day hikers were huddled shivering underneath a rock overhang to escape the driving rain.

Rain turned to hail half the size of my fist and quickly whitened the ground with ice. The temperature dropped into the low 30s, a dramatic fall of more than forty degrees in a matter of minutes. We had waded the stream an hour earlier; it was now eight to ten feet deep and rising, a muddy torrent of rushing water. I tapped a stick into the edge of the flood to check river rise. Within minutes the stick was swept away. At that rate, our cave-like shelter would be underwater in less than an hour.

We had to get out—except *there was no way out.* Uptrail about twenty yards, a cataract of muddy water cascading off the top of the cliff had washed out the trail in a raging floodtide. With the trail cut, we were effectively trapped between the washout, the unscaleable cliff, the rising river, and the sudden extreme cold. Most of us wore only t-shirts and hiking shorts.

The only medical doctor in the group, David checked everyone for injuries and hypothermia. One young man and his wife had brought along their daughters, a little girl about a year old and the other about two. They rode in little seat-packs on their parents' backs.

David took me aside. "We have to get the babies out," he said. 'They'll be in hypothermic shock within a few more minutes."

No one had any dry clothing in which to wrap the kids. A fire was out of the question. I pointed toward the washed-out trail. "That's the only way," I said.

Although, unknown to me, search parties were being organized at the Ranger Station, they clearly wouldn't reach us in time.

"Let's do it," David said.

I am a natural leader, a trait bestowed upon me by God. David had inherited it. The other marooned hikers were looking to David and me for a solution. We explained what we had in mind and how urgent it was to act right away. People glanced nervously at the raging water that had breached the trail. The trail was under four or five feet of foaming fury.

One of the younger, more athletic men stepped forward to help. The three of us herded the hikers to the breach. While they huddled fearfully in the driving rain and hail, I anchored myself with one hand to a small sapling and waded out as far as I could. It required all my strength to withstand the force of the water and not be washed away into the river.

David locked onto my free hand and used me to wade out into the middle of the flood. Rushing water crashed around his chest. Once he became anchored in place, the strain showing in his face, our third man worked past us to the far side and there attached himself to another sapling. Linked together by clasped hands and moored to each side of the washout, we three formed a type of "rope bridge" for the others to use.

Since it was crucial that the two little girls reach shelter as quickly as possible, they and their parents were selected to cross first. The father with the larger child waded out, followed by his wife with the other daughter on her back. The parents' eyes were wide and fearful as they transferred across, stabilizing themselves against the "rope bridge." The daughters were whimpering with fright. The roar of the river to our backs and the waterfall a few feet in front drowned out all conversation.

The mother suddenly lost her footing. She screamed as she and her tiny rider disappeared beneath the roiling water. Her husband wheeled around in alarm. He also lost his footing and went under with the other daughter.

David and I acted instinctively, almost simultaneously. I dived for the woman while David went after her husband. The little family together was being swept into the main river where they would be carried away to their inevitable deaths.

I caught the woman and her baby. The current kept sweeping my feet out from underneath me. I felt myself being carried away with them to deeper, fiercer water. I fought desperately, sputtering and coughing while the woman with the baby on her back clung to me.

Meanwhile, David rescued the father and the other child and managed to re-anchor himself to our third link in the bridge, who was still holding onto his sapling. David, over six feet tall and athletic, braced himself against the water's force and transferred the man and child to safety. Then he reached for me. Our hands locked. We then passed the mother and daughter up onto land.

The family was safe. The three of us reestablished our bridge and helped the other hikers across.

The little girls were still not out of danger. They were shivering uncontrollably. They had to be delivered to somewhere warm quickly before they suffered hypothermia and shock. David and I were both long-distance runners. David took one little girl in his arms, I took the other, and we sprinted with them the three miles back to the Ranger Station.

Local newspapers the next morning credited David and me with saving sixteen people, including the two babies.

"We get into *something* every time I go with you, Dad," David said.

Lord, never hesitate to use me wherever I am needed. Let me have the courage that you displayed at Calvary. And, Dear Lord, thank You for blessing me with sons who possess courage and compassion.

Fishing Tip: The front treble hooks of crank bait often get tangled in your line. Use a one-inch piece of straw-type coffee stirrer to eliminate them. Thread the line through the hollow stirrer and then tie on your lure. The stirrer blocks the line from getting caught and won't hurt the action.

Therefore, my beloved brethren, be ye steadfast, unmovable, always abounding in the work of the Lord, forasmuch as ye know that your labour is not in vain in the Lord.
—*1 Corinthians 15:58*

DETERMINATION

"Nothing in the world can take the place of persistence. Talent will not. Nothing is more common than unsuccessful men with talent. Genius will not. Unrewarded genius is almost a proverb. Education will not. The world is full of educated derelicts. Persistence and determination alone are omnipotent." President Calvin Coolidge.

Determination I have, in fishing or in any other pursuit. I was determined to catch and land a really big shark. Dewey Gubbins and I set out from Port Aransas, Texas, on his 21-foot outboard, bound for the twelve-mile drop-off in the Gulf of Mexico where the offshore oil platforms lined up along the undersea shelf. I got ready the big rods and reels with the eighty-pound-test line while Gubbins turned the boat out into the sea past the long rock jetties. There was a breeze and a short chop.

"Later it'll get rough out," I predicted.

A light sweat greased my skin by the time we reached the twelve-mile drop-off. Gubbins cut a Kingfish in half and used half a fish, or about ten pounds of meat, on each of our shark rigs. The hooks were the size of fish gaffs or hay hooks, attached to sixty-pound steel leaders. The rods with their open-faced reels and 400 yards of line each weighed thirty pounds.

You don't bait-cast a shark rig. I idled the boat across the incoming chop while Gubbins dropped one bait and let out about sixty yards of line. Then he dropped the second bait overboard and I swung the boat ninety degrees into the swell. There was a pencil line of dark cloud on the horizon. The breeze seemed stiffer than when we started out. Swells were troughing out of the chop and the breeze brushed the tops with whitecaps.

"There's a squall coming," Gubbins said.

We anchored with the two heavy baits riding on the bottom fifty yards aft and about sixty yards apart. It was like tightlining for catfish. The heavy rods stood upright in their boots. The tight lines snapped against the grasp of the waves as the boat rose and fell, thudding in the troughs.

Early in the afternoon we had bologna sandwiches and cookies. Other boats were coming in to port ahead of the squall line farther out to sea. I saw rain in strips on the horizon.

My reel in its boot gave a few ticks.

"It's the seas pulling it," I said. "The anchor's broke loose."

"The anchor's holding," Gubbins said.

Ten feet or so of line ticked off the reel. Then the line started to travel slowly through the water, cutting across the stern. Gubbins held onto the side of the boat forward in the cockpit and his eyes followed the line.

"It's not the seas," I said.

"Let him get it good and deep inside his gullet," Gubbins said. "Give him time . Let him take all the slack out of the line and draw it tight. When you feel him, throw all your weight into setting the hook. Then stand by. There's gonna be a fight, bud."

I set the hook. I stood wide-legged for balance on the unstable platform and put everything I had into it. The relentless speed of the line through the water did not change.

"It's not very big," I said.

Gubbins said, "I don't think it knows it's been hooked yet."

Suddenly, the heavy rod bent like I had just roped and goosed a Texas steer. The weight of the shark almost jerked me overboard.

"I was wrong," I said. "It's big. *Big!*"

The reel drag screamed as the fish ripped off a hundred yards of line. A shark is not aerial like a marlin. He fights with honest strength in long, deep, strong runs.

I fought the fish. The muscles in my arms and legs trembled. I pumped when the shark slacked and gave him line when he ran, always making him work against the drag and the stiff rod. I braced my feet against the railing that ran around the boat. I grasped the rod with both hands, trying to gain leverage. I grabbed for things to keep from being pulled overboard.

Gubbins laughed. "Hurry," he said. "The squall's coming!"

The squall loomed near, rain in dark slanted lines with the wind. A freshening wind lapped at my sweaty face. The boat bucked and pitched.

"Don't let him rest," Gubbins said. "Keep up the pressure. We'll have to lift anchor if the squall keeps coming. We'll have to cut your line."

"Don't cut the line," I warned. "I want this shark."

I felt a drop of rain. It felt like a shard of ice on my skin.

The fight went on. "It's been twenty minutes," Gubbins said.

"Thirty minutes," he said later.

The squall rose off our port bow, blotting out the sun. It made the water dark. I was not going to let go.

The shark rose out of the depths like a great gray-winged shadow. A huge blacktip. Gubbins blew a hard breath of astonishment. Then he leaned out over the gunnels, a .357 Colt Python in his fist. The fish sounded. I fought it back to the pistol. It seemed unfair to end the fight like this.

"You'll fall in!" I yelled at Gubbins.

He was leaning far out over the water, straining for a shot. A wave snatched at him. His heels were hooked underneath the seats in the cockpit.

Rain.

A blinding deluge. Immediately, I began shivering. Gubbins yelled into the howl of the storm.

"Get it near the boat," he yelped.

"You'll shoot the boat."

"Bring him close or I'll cut the line."

"Don't dare cut it, Gubbins."
The pistol cracked.
"Missed. Rain in my eyes."
"He's coming back, Gubbins."
I strained on the rod to lift the tired shark's head.
"Good. That's real good."

The shark's jaw snapped open and I saw the vicious rows of teeth and the eyes like a dead cobra's. Rain pelted the seas, and the seas crashed against the boat. We were dragging the anchor. The boat listed coming up out of the troughs. Seas slammed across the stern and for a moment we were knee deep in salt water.

I thought we were sinking.

"Don't cut the line."

Gubbins was coughing. He slung water from his pistol barrel.

"He'll be in the boat with us," he shouted above the fury and the excitement. "Or we'll be with him."

"Gubbins, shoot him. Now!"

He thrust the pistol at the shark and shot it in its small brain.

The blacktip went mad. It only lasted a few seconds. I strained hard on the rod against the last of the shark's fight. Its tail thrashed and it tried to dive through a wave tinged with its own blood. Then it turned belly up and died. The storm thudded it against the side of the boat, and the seas helped wash it aboard.

I tied the huge carcass onto the platform across the stern. It hung off on either side. My head would have easily fit into its open mouth. The nickel-gray skin felt rough one way to the touch, like sandpaper, and smooth the other way. Whitecaps pounded up and rain drummed on the boat. Gubbins in the cockpit waded in water.

But we had my shark.

Later, after I became a Christian, I thought of all the decades of my life when I battled my doubts and sought God with the same tenacity and determination that I fought the shark. I refused to give up in my search for spiritual truth—and out of sheer determination I am slowly unraveling God's purpose for me on Earth.

Lord, I won't give up on You. Please don't give up on me.

> **Fishing Tip:** Double the thrill of fishing for shark. Purchase ribbon fish as bait for Kingfish. Kingfish are fast and wonderful fighters, and good to eat as well. Once you catch Kingfish, use them for shark bait. You can also use hams or other large chunks of raw meat.

Behold, I shew you a mystery...
—*1 Corinthians 15:51*

MYSTERY

From since I was a kid, God has been teaching me to experience and appreciate mystery. I read everything I could find on exploration—Lewis and Clark, Stanley and Livingston, Coronado, Columbus, Magellan, Frank Buck, Martin and Osa Johnson... I often roamed the Ozark Mountains for days at a time, just to see what lay around the bend of the creek, over the next mountain range. When I was about fourteen, a rumor went around that someone had found the track of a Bigfoot, the hairy man-ape of the deep forests. I kicked around in the woods for days trying to find him.

After all, hadn't God created the universe and admonished us to go out and subdue our world—and solve its mystery, if we could?

The Suwannee River, made famous by singer Al Jolson, is one of the most beautiful rivers in the United States. It meanders out of the Okefenokee Swamp in Georgia to curl through cypress, live oaks, palms and palmettos all the way to the Gulf of Mexico near the town of, well, Suwannee. Spanish moss dripping from trees like gray beards lends the river an old man mystical quality. Bigmouth bass in the river are very dark because cypress tannin makes the river the color of coffee.

Kathy, Joshua, our dog Bear and I were canoeing the length of the Suwannee across Florida, camping out, fishing, and swimming in the little clear water springs that feed into the river. Joshua was about four, and already he was a veteran traveler, having ridden "chicken buses" around Mexico, chased wild mustangs in Nevada, went diamond hunting in Arkansas... Every time we climbed into my old pickup, the little blond tyke would tap me on the head with one finger and burst into Willie Nelson's *On The Road Again*.

I caught a good Florida largemouth and saved it for supper just before we entered a section of the river bordered by swamp on either side. An alligator half the length of the canoe sent Bear into spasms of barking as it swam directly across our bow. I whacked it with my paddle and it sounded, leaving only a swirl behind.

The sky in the west began to color for sunset. Kathy had had enough of 'gators for one day. She certainly didn't want to be on the river with them after nightfall. I beached the canoe on a sandbar, the only open ground I could find, and we prepared camp.

Joshua and I built a fire and erected our tent. In the meantime, Kathy breaded and fried the big fish, fried another skillet-full of potatoes, and heated some pork 'n beans. After dinner, the three of us and Bear sat on the sand next to the river and watched night fill up the woods.

I preferred to sleep in the open underneath the stars. Kathy, however, felt more secure inside the tent with the flap zipped tight. We were drifting off when a coarse, deep-throated honk resounded out of the swamp directly behind us. A bull alligator courting a mate. Kathy bolted upright.

"*What's that?*"

"Just a bullfrog," I said quickly. She had already had her share of alligators. "Go back to sleep."

Joshua sat up to listen. "Must be a really huge bullfrog," he decided. "Daddy, let's go see it."

Like me, he was always ready for an adventure.

"Joshua!" Kathy admonished. "You and your dad are not going out there."

But, of course, we did. Kathy wasn't going to be left behind alone. We stood by the dark swamp, listening to the "bullfrog" and marveling over the many mysteries of creation.

"The most beautiful emotion we can experience is the mysterious," the great physicist Albert Einstein once remarked in an interview. "It is the fundamental emotion that stands at the cradle of all true art and science. He to whom this emotion is a stranger, who can no longer wonder and stand rapt in awe, is as good as dead, a snuffed-out candle."

Dear God, I look forward to solving one day the mysteries of the universe, the greatest mystery of all, of course, being You.

Fishing Tip: In a recent poll, 65% of anglers said they find the in-line spinner to be the most productive artificial bait for all varieties of trout.

Delight thyself also in the Lord.
—Psalms 37:4

DELIGHT

"Till you can sing and rejoice and delight in God, as misers do in gold, and kings in scepters, you never enjoy the world."

That was from Thomas Traherne back in the 17th Century. Many years of my life passed during which I delighted in the wonders of God's creation while not rejoicing in God—although I am coming to understand that God and His creations, including man, are inseparable. At certain stages in our lives, I think, God must put us together with special people in order that we learn certain lessons from them. Scotty's pure and good nature helped me to learn to delight in others and ultimately to delight in God.

I met Scott Anderson in Alaska many years ago after we teamed up to hunt caribou when our respective hunting partners couldn't make it at the last minute. A bear of a man with a beard and missing teeth, Scotty owns a small ranch in Colorado and hires out as labor to other farms and ranches and to a livestock sales barn. He is blessed with a warm, simple nature filled with laughter, wonder and delight. Like a child, but not childish. One of my greatest joys is to hear him boom out when I arrive for a visit, "Hey, Chuck! We got a rhubarb pie for you!"

Sandy is his wife. She bakes the best rhubarb pie, the ingredients for which she grows herself. She had the good sense to recognize a gem in the rough when she came across Scotty.

They have two sons. The younger, Cyle, grew up almost as we watched and became a soldier in Iraq. Curtis was afflicted with a rare debilitating disease and died when he was nine years old. I didn't know Curtis, but Scotty told me the story one afternoon while we were fishing a swift trout stream on the

Alaskan tundra.

"You would have loved Curtis," he said. "He knew he didn't have long on Earth, but he was always happy and laughing. People were inspired by just being around him. It was like God and he were always side by side. I've never seen anyone as close to God. He knew he had a better place waiting for him, but he was still going to be happy while he was here."

Scotty made a backpack in which to carry Curtis. He took Curtis with him riding in the backpack wherever he went—hunting, to town, to work on the ranch. Father and invalid son were virtually inseparable. Sandy could hear them laughing and talking as Scotty loped back from the barn or cattle lot with the poor, wasted boy riding on his back. It broke Scotty's heart when he died.

"God gave him to us," he said. "I'm glad we had him for that short time rather than not at all."

It's easy to see where Curtis got his nature. Sandy is warm and gentle. Scotty is a happy, contented man close to the soil and nature.

But he can't fish. In Alaska, I caught enough rainbow and Dolly Varden to feed the entire camp. Scotty flailed the water to a froth—and snagged a rock, two weeds, and my pants leg.

Fishing with him in Colorado, I caught a couple of pan fish while he caught two trees and the back of my shirt.

I own a horse-and-cattle spread in Oklahoma abutting against Flat Rock Creek and Lake Fort Gibson. "Even you can catch fish there," I assured him. "The fish are so plentiful they jump right into the boat with you."

He hooked a boulder, a dead tree stump, twice, and my fishing rod. It was after dark when he, Cyle, and I canoed back from up Flat Rock Creek to beach behind the ranch house. In the moonlight, a school of shad chased by sand bass rippled the surface of the water, leaping and racing for their lives. Suddenly, a sliver of reflected light arced high out of the water and, sure enough, jumped right into the canoe, almost in Scotty's lap.

His laughter thundered across the lake. I envy that in him, his ability to experience delight and simple pleasure in everyday things. Curtis must have had the same gift, truly one from God.

Lord, I pray that I see You in all Your creations and that I delight in You as I think you must delight in those like Scotty, Sandy and Curtis.

> **Fishing Tip:** For best results on springtime bigmouth, fish a spoon on an underwater point by snapping it upward and letting it fall again, working it like this in series from near the shallow top of the point toward deeper water.

The father hath not left me alone...
—John 8:29

COMPANIONSHIP

Llave, whose real name is Keith Laub, liked big fires. He dragged up entire fallen trees and fed them to the blaze, building a flame that reflected off the lake. Tree stumps stuck up out of the fire-reddened water, excellent habitat for Old Whiskers. Earlier, before dark, Llave and I had strung a thirty-hook trout line (or "trot line") across the cove, and now we sat next to his big fire on the shore of the lake and ran the line every two hours.

Llave was a big man, six-and-a-half-feet tall and nearly 300 pounds, with not two ounces of fat on his frame. He and I had been in Army Special Forces together. When we first met, I was a wily old team veteran and he was a twenty-year-old kid with a half-dozen combat knives strapped all over his body. We didn't become friends, however, until years later when Llave was working for an international security agency.

Since I spoke Spanish and was in and out of Latin America as a journalist covering all the little brush fire wars, Llave's company sometimes hired me as a translator and for certain other functions. People often assumed that I must be a soldier of fortune as well as a journalist.

My girlfriend Ana in Tegucigalpa, Honduras, spoke limited English. When I introduced Keith to her, she smiled brightly and demonstrated her English by mistaking *Keith* as "Oh, *Key!*" The Spanish word for "key" is *Llave*—so Keith became *Llave* from that point on.

Llave had a tendency to be domineering, probably because of his size. During our first job together in Latin America, I finally had my fill of his throwing around his weight.

"I can work *with* anybody," I flared, "but I don't work *for* anybody. You're a bully. You're not going to bully me around."

He looked surprised and perplexed, as though no one had ever dared tell him that before. He left the hotel to cool down and was gone for over an hour.

"Chuck, did you really mean that?" he asked when he returned.

"You bet I did. You're a bully."

From that moment on we were partners and close friends. He became one of that select number of people in my life with whom I am completely comfortable and whom I trust completely. As fishing buddies, we were often out slinging baits at bass, but our favorite times were around a campfire while trot-lining for catfish. As with a few others in my companionship circle, we could talk for hours or remain silent for hours with the same sense of ease.

Because of his size, Llave never trusted a canoe. He waited ashore, standing on the bank in the dark with the glow of the fire behind him, while I ran our line.

"Looks like a little channel cat, about a pound or so," I reported.

Kneeling in the bow of the canoe, I pulled myself along with the line from one hook set to the next, rebaiting and removing whatever fish might be on it. I felt something big on the line ahead, putting up a tremendous struggle even before I reached it. I drew in the line with both hands. The canoe bobbed up and down, jerked around in little half-circles. The fish was likely rolling, as big catfish will, twisting the trot line into tangles.

The battle was conducted in sub-darkness, since I was almost out of reach of Llave's firelight. With a final heave, I pulled the monstrous fighting shadow out of the black lake, its weight tipping the canoe dangerously. Water sloshed in on my knees and feet.

I whooped with the thrill of it. The cat had a head nearly as broad as my chest. It was *mad* too and trying to beat me to death while I fought to get it into the canoe. All the splashing and yelling drove Llave into frantic motion. He paced up and down the bank, calling out in his excitement.

"Shoot out here amongst us!" I shouted, using an old comic phrase. 'One of us has got to have some relief."

The catfish's tail boiled the surface of the water and drummed against the side of the canoe. The fish was too long and bulky for me to lift him into the canoe while I was kneeling. I started to stand up to get more leverage, not a wise thing to attempt in the bow of a canoe.

The cat launched its final defensive fire. Breaking free from the hook, it bounced from one gunnel to the next, and the last I saw of it, it was vanishing into the black water from whence I had ripped it. Another big one that got away.

I was soaked with water and shivering from the night air. Llave and I huddled next to his big fire while I dried out, laughing and talking in the aftermath. God has been so good to me, providing me such wonderful times and great companionship and teaching me the value of it.

Grant, Lord, that the companionship I have known with other mortals like myself on earth will be magnified in companionship with You.

Fishing Tip: Anchor the water end of your trot line to a weight that will grant some play in the line to prevent a very large fish from easily breaking free.

> *Whosoever therefore shall humble himself as this little child, the same is greatest in the kingdom of heaven.*
> —Matthew 18:4

HUMILITY

While in Canada bear hunting, D and I borrowed a canoe on a slow afternoon to go pike fishing in an isolated lake surrounded by forested hills. I was about to receive a startling lesson in humility. Pride is a vice with which I've long struggled.

"In reality there is perhaps no one of our natural passions so hard to subdue as pride," Benjamin Franklin wrote. "Disguise it, struggle with it, beat it down, stifle it, mortify it as much as one pleases, it is still alive, and will now and then peek out and show itself."

When I was a paratrooper in Army Special Forces, an artist-friend and member of my A-team sketched me in uniform and green beret with accompanying citation: *When You're The Finest, It's Hard To Be Humble.*

God has blessed me in so many ways. I began life as a ragged little kid in the Ozarks picking cotton—and through the years I've been successful in many endeavors. As cop, as soldier, as academic, as rancher, as freelance professional writer... I'm a proud man. Hopefully, with God's help, I will control my pride and become a successful human being in whom His light shines instead of mine.

A fish has no such concepts of self as pride and accomplishment. Your average fish, in fact, has a brain the size of a BB. Some say your average *fisherman's* brain may not be that much larger. That anglers are so regularly skunked in encounters with them speaks volumes.

D and I were fishing shallow weed beds at one end of the Canadian lake when D's rod suddenly snapped into a hard arch. We knew he had a lunker on the line. Probably a big muskellunge. Muskie are difficult to catch—and often even more challenging to land. A good-sized fish may weigh seventy pounds and reach over five feet in length.

D played the fish. Fortunately, he had it on what I call his "carp pole"—a heavy bait-casting rod and reel with thirty-pound line. A combination like that could jerk the bottom out of the lake. He didn't like to lose a fish once he had it hooked.

The unseen fish gradually began pulling the canoe toward deep water, no matter how I attempted to counter by back-paddling. So swiftly across the surface of the water that we stirred up a wake. There was nothing we could do except go along for the ride. Like the fisherman in Hemingway's *The Old Man and The Sea.*

"This is humiliating!" D cried.

"He's taking us out deep where his buddies can gang up on us," I said.

We laughed so that tears filled our eyes and our sides ached. Was man so much that he could be dragged around like a bobber by a creature so lowly as a fish? God does have a way, at times, of putting us in our places.

D's carp line snapped after about five minutes of being helplessly towed by the great fish. We never once caught a glimpse of it. I think we were both secretly glad that so noble a beast escaped.

I pray that the Lord will continue to seed my way with such fish in order to curb my pride. "For whosoever exalteth himself shall be abased; and he that humbleth himself shall be exalted. (Luke 14:11)

Fishing Tip: For more success with jigs, try attaching a small silver spoon (1/10-ounce, with the treble removed) on monofilament about 2 ½ inches up from the jig. This combination works especially well in shallow water where pan fish are feeding aggressively.

> ***By this shall all men know that ye are my disciple, if ye have love one to another.***
> —John 13:35

LOVE

Everything you love is what makes life worth living.

I know also that Jesus commanded us to love one another. However, my heart had hardened as a result of witnessing death, crime, and violence for some fourteen years as a cop in Miami, Florida, and in Tulsa, Oklahoma. Hardened against people, and against God.

I'm not sure, now, that I knew what love was during that period. There was no room for anyone in my heart after my wife Dianne divorced me and took our two sons fifteen hundred miles away to Florida. No one could take their places.

Not even a little blond boy who needed a father.

Joshua was one year old when I married his mother Kathy. The three of us moved together into "The Tool Shed" on the Illinois River in eastern Oklahoma to "homestead" while I worked at becoming a fulltime freelance writer. One of the first full sentences Joshua pieced together was, "Mommy, I love you."

One day he toddled up to me with his diaper drooping the way it did. "Daddy," he said, tugging at my trouser leg. "Daddy, I love you."

I looked down upon the wide-eyed little boy. I didn't need this; I couldn't handle it. I had two sons of my own, once, and now they were gone. I turned and walked away.

"Charles, you don't mind Joshua calling you 'daddy,' do you?" Kathy asked. "You're the only daddy he'll ever know."

"If that's what you want."

It was better than being called *step daddy*.

Homesteading turned out to be the start of a new life free from the human sewers where I had spent so much of my life as a cop. Kathy, Joshua, and I worked happily over the next five years to build a life together on our mountainside. We moved out of The Tool Shed into a *real* house that I built myself on the meadow in front of The Tool Shed.

Joshua toddled out of diapers into jeans and then, one day, to our astonishment, he walked away to catch the bus to school. My dreams of becoming a writer became reality. I was selling to major magazines, and my first novel, *No Gentle Streets*, was published.

Something was also growing in my heart during those years. The ties between Joshua and me did not bind overnight; I wasn't particularly aware of what was happening. Although I never referred to the little boy as my *stepson*, I did not think of him as my son either. Joshua remained *Kathy's* son. My own sons were gone and growing up without me.

Yet, somewhere along the way, the blond youngster and I grew virtually inseparable. Joshua had a 200-pound St. Bernard dog and a ten-pound Nubian goat as pets. Boy, dog and goat took every step I took in constructing our houses. Goat knee-deep in freshly-mixed cement, toddler ghostly gray crawling out of an empty concrete bag, dog barking. They were my faithful construction crew.

"Such-a-big-help, Daddy?" Joshua asked innocently.

"Yeah, Joshua. You're such a big help."

One night when Joshua was in bed, Kathy asked me, "Do you think you will ever consider Joshua your own son?"

How could I answer that. Joshua, although a delight, was *not* my son.

"I love him as if he were my son," I hedged.

Joshua came to value the outdoors as much as I. Kathy resigned herself to the fact that the two men in her life were often going to come home late smelling of fish, wood smoke, wet dogs, and decaying leaves. Our favorite fishing spot was on the nearby Illinois River. By the time Joshua was four, he was as much at home in a canoe as in his own bed.

"Don't forget to put on Joshua's life jacket," Kathy

reminded me whenever we left with the canoe and our fishing tackle.

When Joshua was six, Kathy's relatives pushed her into explaining to Joshua about his biological dad, whom he had not seen since he was eight months old. Until then, Joshua thought of me as his father, no questions asked. Both Joshua and I suddenly felt insecure about it. While I still thought of him as *Kathy's* son, I found to my surprise that I did not want him thinking of me as his *stepfather.*

Joshua began clinging to me, repeating "I love you, Daddy" so often I realized he was afraid I might disappear if he let me out of his sight.

"I'm never going to leave you," I reassured him.

"Are you the same as a father?" he asked tearfully.

"When I met your mother, I met you too. I chose her and I chose you. That makes me your father."

I almost believed it myself.

Then came that fateful afternoon when our neighbor Bill Alton went fishing with Joshua and me—and I lost my stepson to the dark water.

Joshua eagerly helped put in the canoe at the railroad bridge. Bill clambered into the prow, Joshua scrambled into the center, and I took the stern to paddle. We shoved off and rode the current downriver to where the Illinois forked into a backwater of the Arkansas River and there was a lovely place to fish for stripers and sandies. I tied off to a fallen cottonwood extending into the river. The canoe fought its tether while we fished.

The sun reddened out for its evening rites. Bill hooked into a fish that doubled his rod and took his line zinging. Excited over his landing a lunker striper, I half-stood in the little boat to hand the landing net to him at the other end.

My weight on one side of the canoe skittered the craft into a broadside against the current. The canoe capsized.

"*Daddy!*"

I realized with a horrible start that, for the first time since we had started fishing together, Joshua was not wearing his life jacket. It lay on the bottom of the canoe. How had I forgotten?

Suddenly, the river, so tranquil a moment ago, became ominous and threatening. The water was dark and deep, the current particularly treacherous, and Joshua's little blond head was slicing into it.

I leaped for the boy as he started to vanish into the water.

Oh, my God! No! No!

I twisted in midair before I hit the water, reaching desperately for Joshua, knowing that if I missed him the current would take Kathy's son under and sweep him to his death.

I felt his arms underwater go around my neck. I had him! We continued to sink, the current clawing at us. Water pouring out from the bottom of Tenkiller Dam kept the water so icy it stole my breath. I feared I might not be able to fight our way to the surface, fully-clothed as we were.

But I had Joshua. I clutched him to me with one arm and dug my way to the top with the other. When our heads broke the surface, the sun was so red it seemed to be bleeding into the river.

"Daddy! Daddy!"

"Calm down, son," I said. "I have you. Everything is all right now."

And, indeed, it was. From the moment I managed to save Joshua, with God's help, I knew everything was all right. It was a miracle. I'll never believe anything else but that God had a lesson to teach me about love. Having almost lost Joshua struck home that it is love, not blood, that forms the strong ties of human families. Joshua had been my son for years; I simply hadn't accepted it until I saw that precious blond head sinking into the dark water and felt the terror of never seeing him again.

On that day, with its red sun and black river, I saw my stepson vanish forever into deep water. It was a *son* I brought back from the river's depths.

I am forever grateful to You, Lord, for giving me three sons and, through them, teaching me how to love again.

Fishing Tip: In relatively-shallow lakes where the river is silted, look for hard-bottom areas to fish for largemouth. The best places are man-made rock piles or jetties, or areas where a current washes in and keeps the bottom clean.

Mine eyes shall be upon the faithful of the land...
—Psalm 101:6

LOYALTY

Bill McCracken loved to fish. He and I were partners on the Tulsa Police Homicide Detail. We often spent fishing weekends together at a rustic cabin owned by his dad overlooking a private dock and cove on Grand Lake.

While still in his forties, Bill developed a terminal lung disease that required he carry an oxygen bottle with him wherever he went. His wife divorced him. His constant companion became a little gray Scottish terrier named Duffy.

Bill and I were fishing off the cabin's dock on a sunny day in early winter, catching so many perch that we simply tossed them up on the dock to flop around until we had a chance to clean them for tonight's dinner. Duffy was having a great time running around barking at them.

Suddenly, Bill cried out in alarm. I spun around just in time to see Duffy tumble off the edge of the dock into the icy water. I laughed at the little dog's clumsiness, thinking little about it. After all, I had never known a dog who couldn't swim. All the pooch had to do was paddle around to the ladder and I would pull him out.

Instead, the little animal sank almost immediately. Either Duffy couldn't swim, an unlikely event, or the cold water had sent him into shock. Either way, he was going down. Frantic, Bill began hyperventilating. He appeared ready to jump into the lake, oxygen bottle and all. A fringe of thin ice glistened around the edges of the water. If Bill stumbled and fell in, he and the dog were both goners.

It's just a *dog*. I'd buy him another.

For over fifteen years Bill and I had been partners and friends, devoted to each other no matter what came along—

gunfights, divorce, illness. How far would I go for our friendship? God, I reflected later, must have been testing my loyalty. If I weren't loyal to a friend, I most certainly could never be loyal to God.

With a shuddering sigh, I flung off my winter's coat. I was still fully dressed and wearing heavy boots.

"Stand back!" I shouted dramatically, and with that leaped into the lake after Duffy.

The shock of the frigid water almost took my breath. Unable to swim, clad as I was in winter clothing, I sank as quickly as Duffy had. My only hope was to grab the dog and fight my way back to the surface within reach of the dock.

The water was murky, but clear enough that I glimpsed a small form desperately struggling for its life about six feet under but within my reach. I grabbed the little canine, tucked him underneath my arm, and with all my remaining strength kicked and clawed toward the surface.

Clothing and boots filled with water threatened to sink me to the bottom of the lake. My lungs burned. I didn't think I was going to make it, but I wasn't about to give up. I emerged with a whoosh of breath and grabbed the first thing within reach—a fishing pole Bill was holding out to me.

I thrust Duffy to safety on the dock and clambered up after him. Bill was all over both of us.

"I didn't jump into the lake for Duffy," I assured Bill later. "I did it for you, partner."

He would have done the same for me had our roles been reversed. In fact, he had risked his life for me on more than one occasion when we were cops together. That's what friends did for each other.

I have learned from You, Lord, that deeds count for more than words. Guide me, Lord, to be as loyal to You for the rest of my days as You have taught me to be to others.

Fishing Tip: One of the few spots in North America where muskies may top 30 pounds is Mayfield Lake, Washington.

Thy faith hath saved thee; go in peace.
—Luke 7:50

FAITH

The entire 12th Special Forces Group would be parachuting onto drop zones (DZs) at either end of the Panama Canal—a political "show of force" disguised as a training mission. Some of the lessons we learned would be used later in Operation *Just Cause* when President George Bush sent American troops to seize dictator Manuel Noriega and bring him to the U.S. to stand trial for drug smuggling.

Departing the continental U.S., the big C-130s carrying paratroopers flew south almost in the ocean spray to avoid Central American radar. Aboard, we rigged in-flight from piles of gear stacked at the aircraft centerline. Standing spread-legged to maintain balance, hunching into 'chute harnesses, snapping on reserves and heavy rucks and padded weapons.

I kept thinking of sharks. Man eating sharks were almost as plentiful off the Central American Pacific coast as they were in Australian waters.

"Sharks'll get you if you drop into the ocean," we were warned during "isolation" at Fort Chaffee, Arkansas.

The image that came to mind was that of how a bass explodes beneath a bug struggling on the surface of a pond, sucking it in and then disappearing in a swirl. I felt sympathy for live bait for the first time since I started fishing as a small boy.

"Don't land in the jungle either," we had been warned. "Jungle trees splinter; you could get one jabbed up your rear end."

I saw Panama below through the open paratroop doors. A bolt of raw electricity strobed, crackling in the night clouds, the ocean reflecting the lightning in quick mirror return. Rain skittered and beaded on the metal aircraft floor. The airplane bounced in the storm. Then it was dark again inside, with only the jump lights throbbing red at the doors. Felber the jumpmaster leaned dangerously far out into the slipstream searching for the marker on the drop zone.

The DZ was a half-moon clearing fronting the sea with rainforest on the other three sides. A fourteen-second DZ. Which meant, in order to safely make the clearing, a team of twelve Army Special Forces jumpers had to go out the doors within fourteen seconds.

In a storm? At three a.m. on the darkest night imaginable? Each of us laden with one hundred pounds of battle gear. Jumping from less than one thousand feet onto a strange DZ we couldn't even see?

"My religious belief teaches me to feel as safe in battle as in bed," General Stonewall Jackson wrote. "God has fixed the time for my death. I do not concern myself about that, but to be always ready, no matter when it may overtake me. That is the way all men should live, and then all would be equally brave."

Oh, to have that kind of faith!

During those years of my living dangerously, I foolishly maintained that I could never accept *anything*, not even God, on nothing but faith. I had to have proof, something tangible, logical. I could see and touch a parachute. I had faith in the pilots and in my teammates to do the right thing for which we had trained. Beyond that? I wasn't sure what lay beyond that.

Lightning continued to web the black sky. Rough air threw us against each other in the plane's belly. Winds gusted seaward, toward the waiting sharks. Spotting fire markers on the DZ, Felber sprang back from the door and pointed.

Stand in the door!

It always stunned me how fast and furiously a stick of paratroopers exited a plane. I hurtled through wet darkness, felt my 'chute rip from its pack. It jerked me up hard in the wind, snapping my legs. I felt rather than saw the full canopy blossoming above my head. Wind howled directly from low clouds over the jungle, pushing me tracking at full speed toward the sharks.

With no time to lose, I toggled the Dash-One parachute into the wind. Another flash of lighting revealed other parachutes swarming around me, like a bed of flying mushrooms lost in the dark. I saw white caps butting their heads against the beach directly below my boots.

In desperation I climbed my front risers like a monkey to spill air out the canopy's back skirt and push me toward landfall. That caused the parachute to lose lift. I hurtled downward through the air, falling hot, but it was my only chance of making the DZ and avoiding a swim with the fish.

I wasn't sure I was going to make it, not until the last few seconds. I sensed rather than saw ground rush. I yanked my toggles to my knees and snapped them free just before I touched down. The 'chute grabbed air, jerked, then deposited me on solid ground. Other parachutes were collapsing all around the edge of the DZ. The sharks would have to do without bugs this time.

Years later, it occurred to me that man without spiritual faith in God is heading for the sharks as surely as I was that storm-lit night over Panama. God is his parachute.

Father in Heaven, You have watched over me all these years, protected me from life's sharks, and been my parachute until I awoke to the reality of faith.

Fishing Tip: Northern Pike, even big ones, seem to prefer leeches and leech imitators, particular in the spring. Soft white or yellow plastic leeches, medium sized, are a top option.

> *Give ear to my prayer, O God, and hide not Thyself from my supplication.*
> —Psalms 55:1

PERSEVERANCE

Reverend Jimmy Layne told this anecdote about new Christians and how it wasn't enough that they be saved in Christ, they also had to be maintained afterwards. What good, he added rhetorically in a fishing analogy, did it do to catch 'em if nobody cleaned 'em?

It took a long time for God to catch me—and it's taking almost as long to clean me afterwards. A spring seeping out of a mountainside and a stream flowing through a lining of cottonwoods and willows in an Arizona desert became a metaphor for God's perseverance. How does a man find God when his life is full of emptiness and bitterness—and why would God keep fishing for him?

We were searching for treasure, an old army buddy and I, in the Superstition Mountains of Arizona. At least the fabled Lost Dutchman's mine and its $200 million in gold was our excuse for being in these lava wastelands, some of the remotest real estate on the North American continent. Actually, we were running away from life.

Mad Dog—his army nickname—was running from an unhappy marriage and from the memories of Vietnam and a society that treated him like a leper when he came home. I was running from the loss of my wife Dianne and our two sons. We plodded along with our backpacks while the sun beat down like an old stove-heated flatiron and temperatures pushed 120 degrees.

Mad Dog stopped on a ridge above me, a rugged figure silhouetted against the coppery sky, unsmiling. "Can you think of a better place than this to go if you don't like people?"

Older than the Rockies, the Superstitions were once active

volcanoes. Grim mountain ramparts loom up to 6,000 feet, veritable monoliths of dacite, rugged and formidable. Boulders the size of houses litter canyon floors. Everything that lives here, it seems, has thorns or fangs. An early explorer called the Superstitions the nearest thing to hell on Earth.

Not that hell frightened me particularly. Closing in on forty, I was an ex-cop, ex-paratrooper, ex-rodeo bronc rider, ex-boxer. I had broken virtually every Commandment and, at the moment, unshaved and dust-caked, I looked even worse than I was. Mad Dog and I were two of a kind, mean old lobo wolves, bound together by chains of disillusionment and anger.

We poked around in box canyons near Weaver's Needle, within sight of which the Dutchman Jacob Waltz supposedly hid the entrance to his gold mine. Nights, we spread our sleeping bags clear of caves and rubble where snakes liked to hunt. I shot rabbits and quail for food. I even brought along a small box of survival fishing tackle. Not that I expected to find fish in the desert—but you never knew.

A night in the Superstitions is like nowhere else on Earth. Spires and promontories and pinnacles surround you in a great black amphitheater where breezes blow all night and temperatures drop by as much as sixty degrees. One night I lay on a high ridge near the Needle listening to wind groaning in the canyons. Gazing up at the stars through the clean desert air, I might have been the first or the last man on Earth. Suddenly, I felt as though I was being thrust skyward toward the stars, like an offering. The feeling was so strong it made me dizzy.

"Mad Dog, do you believe in God?"

Mad Dog snorted. "God wants nothing to do with us. That's why He's left us on this lousy ball of mud hurtling through space till we hit something or something hits us."

I found myself thinking about Jesus and the forty days He spent in the wilderness. Had He known this same night silence under these same remote stars? I had always assumed He chose the wilderness for its solitude, to be alone to think, to pray, to get ready for the tremendous assignment that awaited Him. But now I thought it must be more than that. The wilderness was like life itself: full of grimness and harshness and hostility, but also of beauty and strength and inspiration. Maybe the wilderness was the best place to draw near to God. Maybe that was why Jesus chose it.

Mad Dog and I kept drifting. There were few sounds except the crunch of our boots on slag. Almost too late I spotted the huge diamondback rattler coiled in the game trail, its head lifted, wide as the palm of a big man's hand, red eyes glaring. It buzzed menacingly. I was a goner if those fangs pierced my flesh, isolated as we were in the heat.

Even as my foot descended into that scaly mass, I drew my pistol and killed the snake. Three quick, sharp reports.

Mad Dog stirred. "Somebody must like you," was all he said.

I knew that must be true. All my life, something or *Someone* had intervened each time I stepped to the brink. A sniper's bullet barely missed me. My parachute static line wrapped around my arm when I jumped. A rodeo bronc trampled me in Oregon...

Could Someone have a plan for my life, a plan I had not yet fulfilled?

That afternoon, from high above, we spotted a thin line of emerald winding through the parched brown of the desert. A clear stream fed by a spring in the side of the mountain. Mad Dog and I ran toward it, shouting and laughing and shucking our clothing. We jumped in naked. The water was so cold it nearly took my breath away.

I thought I might catch a few sun perch or maybe even a trout for dinner, but there proved to be no fish in the stream. After making camp, I walked away from the fire to be alone. I thought of the snake and how Someone must really care for me. For the first time in years I felt as though I was not walking in total night. I looked up at the stars and uttered a single prayer of thanks—*if* God existed. God hadn't caught me yet, and I certainly hadn't been cleaned. The "catching" came more than twenty years later.

"I'm ready to try again," I told Mad Dog the following morning.

In the dawn of a new day we tramped south to Whiskey Canyon, onto the flat desert beyond, and then out of the wilderness.

I sometimes think of that little stream running through the desert and how there were no fish in it. And I think of how grateful I am to God that He continued to fish for my soul, even when my life's stream seemed barren.

Thank you, God, for persevering.

Fishing Tip: In using spinner baits, learn what fish forage on predominately in a body of water and match your bait color accordingly—reds and browns for crawfish, white and silver for shad and minnows.

> *Thou will show me the path of life: in thy presence is fulness of joy...*
> —Psalm 16:11

PRESENCE

Homer, Alaska, on the Kenai Peninsula is a traditional fishing village. Piers and moored boats take up most of the spit of land that extends into Cook Inlet. On the opposite side of the bay rises a craggy range of snow-capped peaks, forming background for one of the most picturesque settlements on the North American continent.

Old Alaskan friends Lester and Norma Cobb met Donna Sue, our son Darren, and me for a weekend of halibut fishing. Les was a big game guide during hunting season. He and Norma and their four small children were the last family to claim land under the U.S. Homestead Act of 1862, settling Lost Creek Ranch 150 miles north of Fairbanks near the Arctic Circle. I published their story in *Arctic Homestead* (St. Martin's, 2000).

We set out together in a small cabin cruiser across cobalt-gray seas to halibut waters, with salt spray and a brisk wind in our faces. Puffins squawked from rock upthrusts and male bald eagles circled, their heads like silver in the morning sun. Gulls and terns trailed the boat, shrieking and begging for handouts.

Halibut are strange-looking fish but delicious prepared in traditional English fish-and-chips style. They are bottom feeders that resemble rays: flat with "wings," pearly white on the bottom where the mouth is located, dark on top where both eyes together stare straight upward. On previous trips, my son David, old friend Scotty Anderson from Colorado, and I had landed fish weighing up to 100 pounds.

When God was creating the world, He must have saved the best for last, since Alaska seems the epitome of His work. It is a big, wild land of rugged adventurers and half-tamed people who value liberty and solitude above all else. There is always the sea lovely and gray-blue. Whales rise out of the depths to blow, sleek, dark creatures like living submarines. Sea otters floating on their backs remind me of fat old men bobbing in a swimming pool on Miami Beach. Funny round puffins, albatross, eagles, gulls, terns... The sea and the sky above it can be a busy community.

The best bait for halibut are small squid and octopi. It takes a stout ocean rod and a heavy line to horse one of the big fish off the bottom of the sea and reel it up sixty to seventy feet to the surface. They are not exceptional fighters, but they don't have to be. Their flat forms seem to suck them to the bottom. Bringing one up takes brute strength and patience, a bit like trying to pull a stubborn 600-pound steer across a corral.

I delighted in watching my tiny wife struggle with a fish until her arms arched, but she refused help. Darren caught a nice one and looked totally absorbed and carefree. Les and Norma each landed good fish. I caught an 88-pounder, not too bad.

On the way back in to harbor, I balanced spread-legged on the little boat's fantail and watched the low sun make our wake sparkle. Whales were blowing. Sea otters peered at us with their little hands folded across their chests. Omnipresent gulls and terns were still trying to pick a squabble. Up here in this Alaska land, I always felt God's presence more than I ever did in church. There must be a corner of heaven just like this.

Dear Lord, I see Your presence in Your creations.

Fishing Tip: Research shows that fish are eating plastic baits and dying from them. I suggest using biobaits now being manufactured; they degrade in a matter of two or three weeks, compared to about a year for regular plastic lures.

> *For where your treasure is, there will your heart be also.*
> —Luke 12:34

WEALTH

A girlfriend visited my rented condo in Tulsa when I was a middle-aged bachelor. She was a colonel in the army with a magnificent two-story house. I was an itinerant freelance journalist dipping in and out of war zones around the world covering bloody conflicts for magazines and newspapers. I was much more comfortable fishing in the wilds than attending one of her cocktail parties. She looked around my condo, as though perplexed, before blurting out the first thing that must have entered her mind.

"Why, you don't own *anything!*"

After a moment, she added, "Except all the wonderful memories of the things you have seen and done."

Although it embarrasses me sometimes to admit it, I have little concept of the value of money or wealth. After all, I've always contended that material things do not a rich man make nor a shack or "Tool Shed" a poor man. Rich and poor all end up together naked at the finish line. Didn't Montaigne over 400 years ago say: "The ceaseless labour of your life is to build the house of death?" Didn't Jesus some 2,000 years ago say, "...*Thou sayest, I am rich, and increased with goods, and have need of nothing; and knowest not that thou art wretched, and miserable, and poor, and blind, and naked?*" (Revelation 3:17)

I've had money at times, and been rock-bottom poor at other times. I have published more than fifty books and thousands of magazine and newspaper articles and short stories. After three divorces, I now have Donna Sue, with whom I feel loved and cherished. We built a big two-story house on a ranch stocked with fine quarter horses. Should I entertain the urge to canoe and fish some river for a few days, to backpack into ancient Anasazi ruins, to hunt for Sasquatch in the Pacific Northwest, or jaunt off to cover a war somewhere, Donna Sue blesses me and prays for my safety.

Throughout my years of travel and adventure, I have managed to retain my books, which have grown into an impressive library, as well as mementos from my gallivanting around the world. They are my most cherished possession. What I failed to understand until later in life was that God, through these things, was teaching me the value of inner wealth, peace, and accomplishment.

The upstairs room of our GG Ranch house is designed as a library and what grandchildren now refer to as "The Museum." It accommodates hundreds of unusual and distinctive finds I have gathered from the far corners of the globe, each item complete with its own tale of adventure, intrigue, and mystery. Few have any real value, except within my memory. Who would want, for example, a fistful of Anasazi pottery shards, a hand-hewn oar, a mastodon tooth, a wad of camel hair, a crudely-carved wooden fighting cock, a rusted Egyptian scythe, a chunk of rainforest bamboo, a sled dog harness, petrified wood, the rib bone of a whale, a sea lion skull...?

But the wonderful stories behind everything!

I bear an unusual scar on my hand from an expedition to the Amazon River. Not many American fishermen have been gnawed on by a piranha, the skull of which now dangles from a native's blowgun in The Museum.

I keep a single silver reale to remind me of SCUBA-diving with blacktip sharks off the shores of Costa Rica searching for Sir Frances Drake's treasure.

I ripped the Spanish bullfight poster off a wall after I ran with the bulls in Pamplona. The set of wheel chocks hail from the Kimble County Airport in Texas, a stopover on the record-breaking transcontinental flight I made in a powered parachute ultralite aircraft. The pair of chopsticks remind me of the time I parachuted onto the Korean DMZ as a member of the U.S. Army Green Berets. The handful of shark teeth in the abalone shell almost ended up in my backside in the Gulf of Mexico. The big mounted black bass I caught with my partner and friend Bill McCracken. Fish scales the size of silver dollars came from a monstrous carp I caught on light spinning gear and D netted with a lawn chair...

Iron roses, peacock eggs, pewter knights, a photo of a twenty-pound lobster, a carved wooden boat, an MP brassard from *Desert Storm,* combat boots and jump helmet, a pile of Alaskan jade, a bear skin, caribou hides, a mounted pheasant, a pair of spurs and an old lasso...

Wealth, like beauty, is truly in the eye of the beholder. The girlfriend was correct in assuming, according to her definition, that I didn't own anything. However, what I do own are memories of a life lived fully. And, finally, what God taught me was that such wealth also includes serving Him as best I can. It would appear that the ultimate wealth for this old fishermen, the greatest adventure yet to come, is in Heaven.

I pray God is saving a corner for me in His Museum. Thank You for tutoring me in the proper definition of wealth, which is not of this Earth.

Fishing Tip: Jigs are probably the single most versatile family of lures. They can be fished at any depths with equal effectiveness; they are easy to get into cover; they are effective in all seasons and all water temperatures; and they appeal to big fish and to a variety of big fish.

> *Giving thanks always for all things unto God and the Father in the name of our Lord Jesus Christ.*
> —Ephesians 5:20

THANKFULNESS

Using jib and mainsail at half mast, I maneuvered my seventeen-foot Newport *Gandalf* free of Cow Key Channel and into the deep blue and chop of the Atlantic Ocean. I lifted full sail and set a course against a quartering port wind that swept me around Key West and onto the open sea for the day-long journey to the Dry Tortugas. Sailing a small boat is an endeavor that soothes the soul, the only sounds the slapping of waves against the knifing bow, wind humming in the rigging, an occasional shriek of a gull or tern. The sun burned on my bare shoulders, but sea spray kept me cool.

I noticed soot smudged across the eastern horizon, but still figured I could reach destination before weather overtook me. I threw out a baited handline and trolled for yellowtail or perhaps a dolphin or king for my supper. As a poor struggling writer, I had learned to live off the sea's bounty as much as possible.

By midday the easterly was freshening and I felt rain coming. I was on a long reach and skimming along at a good seven or eight knots. I gathered in my fishing line and cranked in sail to get as close to the wind as I could in order to squeeze out another knot or so of speed.

The soot smudge transformed into a fully-formed squall line and continued to gain on me. Low thunder rumbled. Lightning forked, illuminating the angry black face of rolling clouds. I couldn't turn back now. All I could do was try to outrun it.

I was a by-the-seat-of-your-pants sailor. No fancy gadgets, not even a radio. I navigated with a chart and my old army compass from Special Forces.

My soul was no longer soothed.

The first rain drop struck my cheek like the prick of an icicle, followed by a blast of wind that all but capsized the little boat. In blinding sheets of rain, I scrambled to windward in the cockpit and struggled to reduce sail, just in time to avoid disaster. I threw out a sea anchor and decided to run with the wind rather than take the safer course of heading into it and thereby stalling out for the duration of the storm.

I tied off sails and battened down hatches. Seas were already washing over the boat and sloshing in the cockpit around my feet. Rollers appeared, seven-to-nine foot crests of white-capped fury. *Gandalf* rode to the tops of mountains of water, then dropped into the following trough with teeth-jolting suddenness that lifted me in the air and almost threw me into the drink. I tied myself into the cockpit with a length of line. My rudder threatened to crack against the strain.

It grew so dark with the rain and the black scowl of the storm that I could barely see my greatly reduced jib sail forward. It was whipping and popping like a machinegun. There was no way I could control the boat if my sails ripped. I would be at the storm's mercy. Mother Nature rarely extended clemency.

All I could do was ride it out—hour after hour of bone cold-wet, teeth-chattering terror. I understood now how Jesus' disciples must have felt when the tempest overtook them at sea *"insomuch that the ship was covered with waves."*

At some point, I raised land off my bow—a small key (island) clad in mangroves. I maneuvered to its protected leeward where the seas were much calmer. Even the rain diminished to a sprinkle. I double-anchored, thankful for having reached a haven.

While I stood balanced spread-legged on the foredeck, holding onto a stay and gazing with relief out across the shallows to the welcoming beach, a pair of dorsal fins sliced the water between my bow and anchor lines, attached to them the sinister gray shadows of a pair of sharks each more than eight feet long. I had not been alone out there, I realized later, else I may have ended up in the ocean with these hungry creatures. Jesus was there with me—teaching.

"A thankful heart," said Cicero, "is not only the greatest of virtues, but the parent of all the others."

I am so grateful, Lord, to know that You are there to protect me from the tempests life sends my way.

Fishing Tip: Always check forecasts before venturing out to fish in open water. Prepare an escape plan in the event you are caught at sea or on a lake by inclement weather.

> *So when the corruptible shall have put on incorruption, and this mortal shell have put on immortality, then shall be brought to pass the saying that is written, Death is swallowed up in victory.*
> —1 Corinthians 15:54

ETERNITY

Evangelist Billy Graham once advised, "Don't live as if this life will continue forever. It won't. Live instead with eternity in view."

A ghost town in the deep forests along the Yukon River impressed upon my mind that I wouldn't always be here and that I should consider my own mortality. It's a real shock to be confronted with the certainty that without God there is nothing but void—or perhaps a fiery hell—on the other side.

I am drawn to the North Country, to Alaska and the vast Canadian wilds, the last great wildernesses in the world. Paul Christenson from Whitehorse, the capital of the Yukon Territory, dropped my canoe and me off at Quiet Lake, high in the Big Salmon range. I was going to solo-canoe across the territory and into Alaska, fishing along the way.

"It's a beautiful land," Paul said. "But it is harsh and unforgiving. One moment it can lure you into a calmness that settles the soul. The next it will kill you."

I canoed the Big Salmon River as it cascaded out of the lake in a grade as steep as a ski slope. Fast, frothing and exciting, it twisted through spumes of log jams where carelessness on my part meant a wrecked canoe and my either getting drowned or marooned alone in the forest.

I left snow-capped peaks behind in a day or so as the river dropped out of the high country. Although heavily-forested, the land is surprisingly arid; I wasn't too concerned with weather. It was June and the time of the midnight sun. A kind of greenish dusk settled in the middle of official night, but then quickly lifted into another sunrise. It was never truly dark.

I slept using muskeg moss for a mattress. I heard timber wolves howling, and once saw a pack on a point of land extending out over the river. I awoke nearly every new day with bear tracks around my tent. I spotted moose constantly.

Provisions for the journey consisted of Ramen noodles, loaves of bread, peanut butter and honey. I intended to supplement my diet along the way with fish. Unfortunately, the water was high from snow melt, and murky. I trolled with long lines and jigs. I flailed the water mercilessly every time I camped. I trapped minnows, dug grubs from underneath decaying logs, caught a few grasshoppers—but whatever bait I offered, the fish weren't taking. I caught not a single fish. I dined on peanut butter and honey sandwiches.

The swift and narrow Big Salmon River flowed into the wide and more leisurely Yukon River. One day on my way toward Dawson City, I paddled around a long sweeping bend and blinked in astonishment. For there, high on a bank overlooking the river, in the greenish half-light of a Yukon midnight, out in the middle of nowhere, was a town—a scene as placid and picturesque as a New England postcard.

I beached my canoe, climbed the high bank, and strolled through a silent town where no one lived. A ghost town. About thirty buildings remained: a log church complete with pews and pulpit; a one-room schoolhouse still furnished with its pot-bellied stove, hand-hewn "Little House on The Prairie" desks, and a stretched moose hide for a blackboard; a blacksmith shop; a Hudson Bay general store. Some of the residences looked as though the occupants had just departed, leaving behind all their belongings. Everything remained remarkably preserved because of the arid climate.

Being alone in the wilderness is different from being alone where man has lived and worked and built on his dreams, only to surrender it all in the end. I felt like an intruder prowling where people had just stepped out for a century or so, but would be returning shortly.

The name of the town was Fort Selkirk. I later learned how it was originally settled as a trading post in 1848 by Hudson Bay Company explorer Robert Campbell. The settlement was used for many years by miners, trappers, steam boaters, soldiers, and traders. In 1898, Canada sent the Yukon Field Force to build military camps there and at Dawson to prevent a suspected annexation by the United States during the Klondike Gold Rush.

Typhoid struck, nearly wiping out the town. Two or three families survived and remained in the town until 1951, whereupon they abandoned it to ghosts and time.

The Yukon River afforded the only access to the town, as there were no roads. A main street of sorts cut through the center of the settlement and threaded off into dark woods for about a quarter-mile. It was so rutted by a century of foot, cart, and livestock traffic that nothing would ever grow on it again.

I followed it to an ancient cemetery surrounded by firs heavily burdened with gray moss and lichen. Rough tombstones bore dates beginning in the 1850s, with a sudden proliferation in the 1890s when typhoid struck. Suddenly, the short hairs began crawling at the nape of my neck. I felt as though I were being watched, not by an animal, nor by a man, but by *something*. I don't believe in ghosts, but I still used up all my reserves of self-discipline to keep from bolting back down the road like a spooked teenager. The souls of typhoid victims in their graves may not have been at rest.

All those people buried there had once lived and thrived in this picturesque little village. Now, there was nothing left of them after all these decades except ghosts. No one left to remember them. Theirs, I concluded, was a fate prescribed ultimately for all of us. What panicked me, perhaps, was my sudden and unexpected confrontation with eternity. I couldn't help asking myself, *What happens on the other side?* Do we live for a comparative instant, the snap of our fingers, and then vanish, leaving nothing behind but old ruts and tombstones overgrown with weeds and time?

I returned to the river bank to fish and not think about it. I would think about it later.

Lord, help me to understand and live for Your eternity beyond these short mortal years on Earth.

Fishing Tip: A snagged lure is inevitable when fishing heavy cover. To free it, "crack the whip" by lifting your rod tip to the ten o'clock position, tighten the line, sharply snap the rod tip downward, then immediately flick the tip upward to nearly vertical. This action, compared to snapping someone with a wet towel, puts sudden pressure on the lure and often rips it free.

Be strong and of a good courage, fear not...
—Deuteronomy 31:6

COURAGE

The Florida Everglades is a vast sea of grass broken by the occasional palmetto hummock and veined with natural canals, swamps, and waterways. Les Wheeler, a fellow Miami cop, and I ventured forth into the Glades one morning for a day of bass fishing, penetrating deep and portaging our boat to where big, dark-colored bass were plentiful.

Using either plastic worms or swimming minnow lures, we hooked into an abundance of two- and three-pounders, with the occasional four- or five-pounder. We kept only those bass we could use for the table, releasing the others.

The day seemed to pass in an hour, so absorbed were we in fishing. Les netted a fine catch, then looked up and said, "Uh-oh!"

The western sky glowed red and purple with approaching sunset, tingeing the tops of water grasses with scarlet and turning the dark waters to flame. *Uh-oh* meant we had overstayed. Les cranked up the outboard and we went for a fast ride, weaving across the Everglades like on a Disney World ride.

Night comes quickly in the tropics. One moment it is daylight, the next it is dark. The moon would rise late tonight. Only the stars and the distant glow of Miami guided our way. We faced at least three portages across swampland in order to return to civilization, each of which was anywhere in distance from a few hundred feet to a few hundred yards.

In portaging, we rammed the boat through reeds that towered above our heads, then as far up on dry or semi-dry land as we could get it. Visibility was all but nil in darkness that defied definition. Pulling the light river boat through the grass, we used our free hands to beat the way ahead with paddles to scare away critters. Alligators scrambled out of our way. Poisonous cottonmouth snakes as thick as our forearms slithered and hissed.

In this spooky manner, we made each portage and worked our way toward the horizon glow of the city, toward the light. Later, it occurred to me what God was teaching. Life without God is a vast darkness filled with obstacles and dangers. Only belief and faith in Jesus can safely illuminate our journey toward the light.

"Tis true that we are in great danger," Shakespeare wrote. "The greater therefore should our courage be."

Be my light, Lord, beckoning and guiding me out of worldly darkness.

Fishing Tip: In night fishing, it seems a night of really hot fishing in a particular location is usually followed by several marginal nights. Apparently, fish come in to a spot to feed, then don't feed there again for the next three or four days.

> *The blessing of the Lord, it maketh rich, and he addeth no sorrow with it.*
> —Proverbs 10:33

BLESSINGS

I cut two willow saplings about eight feet long. To the limber end of each I knotted a length of monofilament. I attached to the business end of each line a Coachman trout fly in black and red, a color combination I found worked well for rainbow in high country. I handed one pole to my grandson Cass and kept the other for myself.

"You have to catch your dinner—or you don't eat," I teased.

Cass and I were backpacking the Colorado Rocky Mountains, kicking around together in the wilds for a few days. Cass was sixteen. In another couple of years he would be going to college and then out into a life of his own away from The Ranch. After that he wanted to enlist in Army Special Forces (the Green Berets) and then go into law enforcement. I wanted to spend some time with him, share with him my love of nature and of the God who created such beauty.

Armed with our willow poles, we worked a small icy stream tumbling out of snow melt higher up. It beat itself frothy over rocks and through chutes, pooling here and there in dark shade in the calmer, deeper waters at the bases of boulders. That was where trout hung out.

Laughing and shouting, caught up in the moment and the endeavor, we soon hooked several pan-sized rainbow trout sparkling in the high-mountain sunshine. Firm, lively fish from cold water. A 100-pound halibut or a twenty-pound land-locked salmon could not have been more welcome.

Together, Cass and I built a small fire. From our packs we took a camp skillet, some butter and corn meal, and a can of pork 'n beans. Cass cleaned the trout. I battered them with corn meal, got butter hot in the skillet, and dropped in the rich slabs. The appetizing aroma of fresh frying fish added zest to the scent of pine needles and clean air.

We ate our fill. I leaned back against a rock ledge in the sunlight and, eyes half-closed with contentment, reflected on all the blessings God had bestowed upon me over the years. I was indeed so very rich in the wealth that counted most—backpacking with a grandson I loved and catching trout high in the Rocky Mountains. Many a Scrooge had filled his coffers while starving his soul.

The Chouteau Hills Church of Christ near our GG Ranch in Oklahoma publishes a little monthly pamphlet called *House To House, Heart To Heart*. I thought about an article I had read in it that ought to be required reading for every American, for it put into perspective exactly how blessed we in America really are:

WE'RE SO BLESSED

If you own just one Bible, you are abundantly blessed. One-third of all the world does not have access to even one;

If you woke up this morning with more health than illness, you are more blessed than the million who will not survive this week;

If you have never experienced the danger of battle, the loneliness of imprisonment, the agony of torture, or the pangs of starvation, you are ahead of 500 million people in the world;

If you can attend a church meeting without fear of harassment, arrest, torture, or death, you are more blessed than three billion people in the world;

If your parents are still married and alive, you are very rare, even in the United States;

If you have money in the bank, in your wallet, and spare change in a dish someplace, you are among the top eight percent of the world's wealthy;

If you have food in the refrigerator, clothes on your back, a roof over your head, and a place to sleep, you are richer than seventy-five percent of this world.

I am so grateful for Your blessings, Lord, and even more grateful that you have taught me how to appreciate them.

> **Fishing Tip:** Each year, hundreds of anglers suffer heart attacks while indulging their sport. If you have had heart problems of any sort—or even if you haven't—always carry a bottle of aspirin in your tackle box. It can save your life. Aspirin is a blood thinner as well as an analgesic. Quickly swallowing an aspirin at the first symptoms of a heart attack helps restore blood flow and prevents further blood clots from forming.

Which of you by taking thought can add one cubit to his stature?
—Matthew 6:27

PERSPECTIVE

I keep scrapbooks that document my life and that of my family on my mother's side. I know virtually nothing of my biological father other than that he was a half-breed Creek Indian. I have many typical "big fish" photos: mugging into the camera while holding a big fish or a string of big fish. Northern Pike in Canada; halibut in Alaska; salmon in Michigan; sharks in the Gulf; trout in Colorado; channel cat on the Mississippi River...

Like most anglers, I take the photos at the time because I'm excited. But then I place them in my scrapbook and forget about them. God, it seems, has a way of putting things into the proper perspective whenever I begin to think I may be more than a mere part of His creation clinging for an all-too-brief span of time to the crust of a big ball hurtling through space. Such as, for example, the time *I* became the "big fish" for the camera.

For years, part of my daily routine has included a five-mile run. One morning I was chugging contentedly along when an old rusted Mercury full of fat women pulled up alongside and stopped. I was dripping sweat and wore only running shoes and cut-off jeans.

"Are you Charles Sasser the writer?" one of them asked out the car window.

"Well...yes."

Whereupon, four hefty dames armed with a Brownie camera piled out of the car and took turns posing with me. Throwing their arms over my perspiring shoulders and around my waist as though we were old buddies. Like anglers posing with a prized catch.

Then they jumped back into the Mercury without so much as a by-your-leave and roared off in a cloud of dust. It's a challenge to think of yourself as more than you are when you know that, somewhere, strangers are holding you up on a stringer in a photo.

Dear God, empty me of vain conceit, excessive pride, and selfish ambition. Remind me that my goal should be to end up on Your stringer.

Fishing Tip: *When rivers start to clear after spring rains, backwaters will clear up first and bass there will hold deeper than they will in stained waters.*

Trust in the Lord, and do good; so shalt thou dwell in the land, and verily thou shalt be fed.
—Psalms 37:3

TRUST

"*Tenga confianza,*" Iris said. "Have trust."

She had asked me to go fishing with her. But not *just* fishing. "We will *call* the fish," she promised.

Right. I had been snipe hunting before.

Iris was young and brown-skinned and pretty. A *Tico,* a native Costa Rican, who had grown up in a large family of jungle people in the Osa rainforests along the Sierpe River.

Like the snake for which it is named, the Sierpe meanders through tropical jungle before it erupts into Drake's Bay on the Pacific Coast. Tides, currents and strong wave action combine to stopper up the mouth of the river and back water up into a wide swamplands infested by caiman, snakes, and varieties of fish. Iris and I paddled her wooden dug-out canoe, called a *pirogue,* into the slough of giant trees, lianas, and gray-dripping moss. Her eyes constantly darted, searching.

Suddenly, turning to flash one of her bright smiles at me, she pointed to a bushy tree growing in the water. The tree produced a strange-looking crop, like a hybrid cross between a nut and a berry. She indicated I should tie up to it.

"Well," I challenged. "Start calling."

To my astonishment, that agile jungle girl scampered up and into the branches of the tree. The next thing I knew, she was hooting like a troupe of monkeys and shaking the tree. A hailstorm of the strange fruit dimpled the brackish water all around the *pirogue.* Large red snapper began boiling the water as they fed on the harvest. It wasn't long before we had a good catch.

Everything made sense once I thought about it. Monkeys also like the fruit of the strange tree. Whenever they congregated to feed in one of the trees, hooting and creating a disturbance, they shook loose some of the fruit, which fell into the water and attracted fish. Thus, in effect, Iris was actually *calling* the fish, playing out an ages-old symbiosis between man and God's other creatures. The natives trust in God to provide for their needs if they but understand how his creations work.

"*Tenga confianza.*"

"*And He said unto them, Cast the net on the right side of the ship, and ye shall find. They cast therefore, and now they were not able to draw it for the multitudes of fishes.*" (John 21:6)

I know, Dear Lord, that You will provide all that we need if we but put our trust in You.

Fishing Tip: Want to squeeze more storage out of your tackle box, without tangling your hooks? Glue small pieces of foam carpet padding to the bottoms of the trays to hold hooks in place and thus provide more storage without the problem of tangling your spoons, spinners, and other baits.

For I have learned, whatsoever state I am, therewith to be content.
—1 Timothy 6:6

CONTENTMENT

All hearts have in common the need for beauty, and for contentment. Music, reading, gardening, or any of a variety of other pursuits fill that need for some. God taught me as a child to be content in life's simple things and to relish the natural beauty that surrounds us. I required so little. Nothing more than, for example, a catfish.

The "Ticky Place," so-called because the area was infested with the parasites, supported a small stream in a woods of blackjack oak, maples and thorned locust. The house was a weathered unpainted shack without insulation or inner walls. We tacked up old newspapers and cardboard to keep out the winter winds. Snow blew underneath the door and crusted on the worn linoleum halfway to the wood-burning stove.

A kitchen took up one end of the house, the living room the other, with a closet-sized bedroom between. Mom and my step dad slept in one bed, my two brothers and I in the opposite one, with a narrow walkway separating them. Closets consisted of lengths of baling wire stretched above the beds, to which we hung our clothing.

Rent for the Ticky Place amounted to ten dollars *a year.*

I often collected wild creatures and made pets of them. Crows, hawks, squirrels, dove, raccoons... Relatives noted how I was an odd kid in that I often preferred the company of critters over that of most people.

I caught a nice catfish while fishing with Paw in Sallisaw Creek. Normally, we ate everything I could catch or shoot, whether fish, 'possums, squirrels, or 'coons. For some reason, however, I kept the catfish and dammed up a section of the stream about a hundred yards from the house to make a large pool for its home. I caught grasshoppers and dug worms to feed it. Soon, it was taking bait from my fingers. It grew to about two pounds in size before the end of the summer.

On the far side of the stream was a grassy knoll that quickly rose into a copse of maples and cedars. On the knoll I constructed a tent-shelter from an old scrap of canvas. When the sun shone, I lay on the grass next to the pool and watched my catfish. When it rained—I loved summer rains—I crawled into my lean-to, drew up my legs, and sat there completely content and at peace with the world while I listened to the patter of raindrops on canvas and watched the dimpling of my private catfish pond.

A child can live more life in a single afternoon than an adult can in a lifetime. God must surely have been speaking to me, teaching me to value the contentment which no amount of money or success can provide. I still relish lying in the sun, sleeping in a tent in the rain, or sprawling next to a creek to daydream away the day.

I also have a special affinity for catfish.

Lord, no matter how much success You have allowed me in my endeavors, I thank You must for teaching me to be content with the simple beauties of life. It is Your truth that we don't really develop our core convictions so much as they develop within us when we are young.

Fishing Tip: Your favorite spinning reels will cast farther and last longer if they're buffed at least twice a year.

He will swallow up death in victory; and the Lord God will wipe away tears from off all faces...
—Isaiah 25:8

DEATH

We rented a vacation condo in the Florida Keys for a family holiday: my wife Donna Sue and me; son Darren; daughter DeAnn and DeAnn's husband Kenny; their sons Brandon, Cameron, and Skylar. For a week we fished the surf or rented a boat to snorkel and fish in the cuts between the Keys. That was the last vacation we were to have with DeAnn. She died soon after in a car crash; she was only 34-years-old. None of us knows what tomorrow may bring.

Donna Sue's heart was breaking, bringing a sadness that would remain in her soul for the rest of her life. Nonetheless, her spiritual strength, her belief in God and Heaven transcended all grief, a strength that was an inspiration for a tough man like me. She stood up and faced trouble and sorrow, whereas I often ran away from hurt—off in a canoe to some lonely waterway, on a horse into the high country.

Donna Sue wanted her daughter buried near us on our ranch. We selected an open meadow overlooking a pond and, in the distance, the shores of the lake. Darren and I dug the grave with shovels and picks. I was in the bottom of the hole working when Skylar unexpectedly appeared. He was three years old.

"Pa-Pa?"

Startled, I looked up. The little boy was on his hands and knees looking down at me from the lip of the grave.

"Is that where we are going to put Mommy?" he asked.

I collapsed, blubbering incoherently, devastated by the anguished look on the child's face. Darren helped me out of DeAnn's grave. I hugged my tiny grandson to me and carried him away from the meadow. I couldn't understand death myself, not completely; how was I going to explain it to a little boy?

I know only that You, Lord, have promised that those who believe in You shall never die. "O Death, where is thy sting? O Grave, where is thy victory?" *(I Corinthians 15:55)*

> **Fishing Tip:** Nothing heals sorrow like fishing a quiet stream where God's presence is all around.

And immediately Jesus stretched forth his hand and caught him, and said unto him, O thou of little faith, wherefore didst thou doubt?
—Matthew 14:31

CURIOSITY

Albert Einstein: "The important thing is not to stop questioning."

James Thurber: "It is better to ask some of the questions than to know all the answers."

Charles Steinmetz: "No man really becomes a fool until he stops asking questions."

Jesus: *"For every one that asketh receiveth; and he that asketh findeth; and to him that knocketh it shall be opened."* (Matthew 7:8)

A child's favorite word is "why."

"I want to know everything," I told my mother. "Why *can't* I know *everything?"*

Existential curiosity about the universe and my place in it raged within my soul whenever I was alone in the wilderness, which was often as a youth. Fishing at night on the banks of some quiet waterway, I would lie on my back in the dark, fishing pole propped on a forked stick, and gaze up into the universe. I was obsessed with space, infinity and eternity. Perhaps somewhere out there—if I could just make it *out there*—I would actually *see* God, if He existed.

It wasn't that I doubted the existence of God so much as it was that I could not understand the meaning of it all. Even so, there are many references to doubt and to curiosity in the Bible. Simon, Peter, Nicodemus, Zacharias, Moses, and many others expressed their doubts and curiosity about God, Jesus, and all things spiritual. Jesus Himself invited us to be curious—for out of our curiosity we will seek answers.

When man first walked on the moon in 1969, I was an

over-the-hill retread student of History and Anthropology at Florida State University. I stayed up all night to watch the walk played over and over again on TV. I snapped pictures of it off the screen. Maybe we could find answers to my questions now that mankind was exploring the universe.

In 1985, I thought I might actually make it out there among the stars into whose immensity I had stared from creek banks most of my life, wondering. I was a finalist for NASA's "Journalist-in-Space" Project, which meant I had an excellent chance of flying into space to see for myself.

"Why do you want to go?" a member of the final selection panel asked me.

"To see," I responded immediately. "To experience. To go where so few others have gone. To be among those who take first tentative steps off this planet on journeys to put footprints on the stars. And then to write so others may experience it through me."

The Challenger disaster in January 1986, in which seven astronauts were killed, including "Teacher-in-Space" Christa McAuliffe, ended NASA's civilian program. No journalist would fly. I was devastated. I actually had a chance.

Many who question God seek to get their spiritual groove on by placing stones on their chakras, striking yoga positions, channeling the dead, consulting horoscopes, runes, tarot cards, and palm readers, or chanting to Buddha while barbecuing hot dogs with the neighbors.

My curiosity led me to explore the idea behind Intelligent Design, which presupposes, logically, that supreme intelligence *has* to be behind the creation of the universe. All this we see did not occur by accident. Life as we know it did not emerge as microorganisms from the primordial muck to become ACLU members.

"You will find me," Jesus promised, *"when you seek me with all your heart."* (Jeremiah 29:13)

I was almost sixty years old and making a record-breaking transcontinental flight in an ultralite powered parachute aircraft when, almost as a miracle, I suddenly received the answer to many of my questions. Seeking was finally paying off.

I still lie on creek banks staring up into the stars while I fish—but now there's one great difference from before. I no longer ponder *what*. Now I wonder *how* and *what will it be like?* when I get up there and can ask all my questions of the Great Prime Mover Himself.

Dr. Francis Collins, renowned scientist, director of the Human Genome Project, and a Christian, had this to say: "Reason alone cannot prove the existence of God. Faith is reason plus revelation, and the revelation part requires one to think with the spirit as well as the mind."

Father, when my curiosity gets the better of me and I lie on a creek bank gazing up into Your universe, please remind me of Your truth and take me back to the basics of believing.

Fishing Tip: Three blades on a bait are better than one when you're fishing spinners at night.

> *And God created great whales, and every living creature that moveth, which the waters brought forth abundantly, after their kind, and every winged fowl after his kind: and God saw that it was good.*
> —Genesis 1:21

ABUNDANCE

A sea bass half the length of my forearm darted for cover, scattering a school of bright orange Garibaldi. I gulped a deep breath through my snorkel, doubled at the waist, and shot after it, using my fins as thrusters. Moments later, I surfaced with the bass pinned to the spear of my Hawaiian sling. Honest Abe grinned.

"*Este pescado son delicioso para la cena,*" he said. Indeed, it would be great for supper.

"God always provides from His abundance," one of the other Mexicans on the research team assured me.

Abrams, whom I dubbed *Honest Abe*, was an oceanographer with the University of Mexico. I was in-country with him and nine other American and Mexican scientists and students to conduct research on sea lion diets and what impact they might exert on Mexico's fishing industry. We were camped in tents at Gran Canon on the southeastern shore of Cedros Island in the Pacific Ocean, offshore of Baja. Since Honest Abe and I were the most experienced divers of the group, we provided fish, lobster and octopi for evening meals.

The largest of Mexico's Pacific islands, Cedros is 21 miles long and nine wide. When the Spanish discovered it in 1540, they mistook stunted forests of pine and juniper growing in the mist along its spine for cedars. Thus the name, *Cedros.*

A variety of wildlife inhabited the island, including lizards, horned toads, freshwater frogs around the springs, foxes, cottontail rabbits, rock squirrels, a small species of mule deer, and a rare pink rattlesnake. One of the tiny, odd-colored vipers was lying coiled in the sand at the low entrance of my tent one morning when I crawled out on all fours.

Life for the fishermen who inhabit the single village on the island revolved around the fish cannery, which perched above an idyllic cove filled with small seagoing fishing boats called *pangas*. While the fishermen were at sea, the women worked the cannery and the children attended school. The principle sea crops were varieties of fish, octopi, and abalone, a large shell fish whose meat was much prized by seafood and gourmet restaurants. Japan imported the polished shells to make into such delightful creations as jewelry and inlaid coffee tables.

Air compressors and the outboard motor have made the Mexican abalone fishermen's fate somewhat easier, but their lives were still hard and dangerous. Abalone clung to the ocean floor at depths of twenty to one hundred feet and more. Fishermen worked in three-man teams. One operated the boat, one tended the air compressor that pumped air to the third, who walked on the sea floor using a pry bar to rip the shellfish free of their rocky underwater perches.

I never heard any of the fishermen or their families complain of their hard lot in life. Most were quick to praise God and light a candle for the abalone He provided. Honest Abe and the research team were on Cedros to do what we could to make sure the proliferation of sea lions did not eventually starve out the fishermen.

The Pacific is cold water, unlike the warm Sea of Cortez between Baja and the mainland. I wore at least the top of a wetsuit whenever Abrams and I went fishing. Nonetheless, I was always shivering by the time we scared off sea lions in order to bag a few *corvina,* octopi and lobsters.

An octopus is easy to catch. You dive down to where octopi are stuck in the shadows underneath rock ledges and feel around until you find one. You insert your fingers into its air holes and turn its head inside out. Thus disoriented, the octopus will cling desperately to anything within reach. Clamp it onto your shoulder, your arm, or your leg and it will stay there, no matter what, until you remove it in time for dinner. Cooked with rice, it tastes a bit like boiled rubber bands.

Some of the largest spiny lobster ever caught have come from these waters. One afternoon we pulled out a twenty-pounder. Our designated camp cook steamed it, even its antenna, which were as large as average lobster tails, then added fried fish, rice and octopi, and flour biscuits. Everyone congregated in a circle to eat, sitting on rocks. One of the Mexicans gave thanks to God for providing.

People who have so little are nonetheless grateful for the abundance God provides. There is a lesson there for all of us spoiled by plenty.

Dear God, may I never take for granted that which You provide so abundantly.

Fishing Tip: About seven miles off the Gulf Coast of Port Aransas, Texas, is a sea ledge near the offshore oil rigs where large blacktip shark hang out. Tightline for them as you would for catfish, using the largest hooks you can find, stout sea rods, and five-pound chunks of Kingfish for bait.

Provide things honest in the sight of all men.
—Romans 12:17

HONESTY

Fishermen enjoy a reputation, perhaps justifiably, for telling whoppers bigger than any whopper they might catch. It's all in fun, adding an inch or two to the size of that cat hooked along the rip-rap below the dam. Okay, maybe a foot or two. I found myself caught in a true ethical dilemma while fishing in the Great Lakes region.

"For we have made lies our refuge, and under falsehood have we hid ourselves." (Isaiah 28:15)

Swift and cold describes the Muskegon River where it thrusts past Newaygo on Michigan's lower peninsula and slices its way toward Lake Michigan. The autumn foliage was bright and I was knee-deep in the river, busy with one of the largest, fightingest, most exciting fresh water fish in the world.

"You haven't lived until you hang into a hog salmon with a light outfit," my wife Kathy's uncles, Bob and Richard Deatherage, had challenged.

They were right. My lunker turned out to be a 28-pound King salmon, a hard-pulling, strong-running fish. It would strip line from my reel, then freight-train toward the surface and explode out of the water in a spectacular aerial display of strength and grace. Three feet of power leaping into the air again and again.

And people said spawning salmon wouldn't feed once they got into the rivers, wouldn't hit. The truth is—*they won't feed.* In spite of that, and although snagging was illegal except at a few limited sites, anglers harvested thousands of the big fish each year. How did they do it without breaking the law?

"The salmon no longer eats or is even capable of digesting food when it enters our rivers to spawn," declared Ray Ferguson, President of The Salmon Association of Michigan, "hence the relative ineffectiveness of bait or artificial flies or lures."

Encyclopedia Americana notes how, "Their throats and stomachs become entirely incapable of receiving food, and the desire to feed leaves them entirely."

Still, outdoor sports magazines constantly published spreads of sportsmen hooking into fighting landlocked salmon. How were they catching fish that refused to strike?

"When in rivers," wrote one angler, "salmon eat little or nothing, but are sometimes hungry enough to grasp at an angler's bait."

Sounded reasonable. I'd have to find *hungry* salmon.

Another insisted, "Brightly-colored spoons, spinners and streamers are all nuisance items that are fair game for a spawning salmon's short temper."

Good. I'd make 'em *angry*.

"Annoy a salmon enough times by dazzling a fly in front of his nose," advised yet another sportsman, "and he will drill it."

I'd *dazzle* 'em.

"Run crank bait with mind-maddening action into areas containing fish," suggested still another, "and they will finally smash lures out of frustration."

Frustrate 'em. That was the secret.

I saw my first King as the Deatherages and I were setting up camp. A man came grinning up from the direction of the river lugging a gigantic fish whose tail dragged the ground.

"What'd you catch him on?" I asked.

He cast me a suspicious look, then quickly opened the salmon's mouth to show me hook marks.

"A blue Cleo," he said. "Nailed him right there. See where the hook was?"

I had *never* had a bass angler or a Muskie fisherman show me hook marks. Who cared if you caught it in an upper or lower jaw? I concluded the angler didn't want me thinking the fish was illegal, since snagging was outlawed. I didn't say anything about the other hook marks on the big fish's back.

Later, I spotted similar marks on the bodies of other fish. Invariably, each fisherman passionately advocated some lure or other and showed me hook marks in his fish's mouth. A lot of fish were being caught. I could barely contain my enthusiasm.

The next morning on a swift river masked by autumn fog, I began my experiments to entice a big salmon to hit. I could see them darting about in the clear water, hovering over their beds, or struggling in the rapids with their huge tails and dorsal fins protruding above the water's surface. I anchored over salmon beds and teased the fish with every bait in my tackle box. I jiggled jigs in front of their noses, dropped Cleos in their beds, reeled baits among them with mind-maddening action. I teased 'em, annoyed 'em, frustrated 'em, and dazzled 'em. The salmon wouldn't even look at my offerings. Their entire nature was directed toward one goal—spawning.

It annoyed me to hear frequent shouts of excitement from other boats as someone tied into a large fish that went tail-walking across the water. Finally, I was frustrated enough to give up.

"The only way you can catch 'em," I groused, "is to snag 'em with the lure!"

Bob Deatherage grinned. "Now you've caught on."

I stared. "These people are catching fish illegally? They're just pretending to be legal? That's hypocritical."

"It's also the only way to catch river salmon. You foul-hook 'em, mark their jaws with your hook, and pretend you caught 'em fair. That's the way it's done. Otherwise, maybe one in a thousand would ever catch a single salmon out of this river."

I began to catch fish, having fallen into the trap of hypocrisy and outright lies that cloud all anglers who go for the fall run of land-locked salmon. Anyone who caught a salmon was a snagger and therefore an outlaw, since the fish could not be caught by conventional rod-and-reel means. Even law enforcement officials went along with the duplicity. As both an ex-cop and someone who valued honesty, how could I have participated in all good conscience?

Afterward, I was ashamed that I let myself succumb to the chicanery. In an effort to rectify the situation as it existed, I exposed it in a controversial article I published in *Great Lakes Fishermen*. I never went salmon fishing again in the rivers of the Great Lakes.

Dear God, I know it's sometimes difficult for lowly man to live up to the standards You have set, but with Your help and grace I will continue to try to be honest to myself and to You in all things.

> **Fishing Tip:** To catch land-locked salmon in the Great Lakes, go early before the migrations start. Salmon go into a feeding frenzy in open water just before they swarm into the mouths of rivers. This is when they'll strike almost anything—and it's both honest and legal.

The spirit of a man will sustain his infirmity; but a wounded spirit who can bear.
—Proverbs 18:14

SURVIVAL

In the April 1998 issue of *Outside* magazine appeared an article about a 70-year-old man named Dick Person who lived in a teepee in a remote corner of the Yukon Territory as a hunter-gatherer. "Once you develop a certain level of competence," he said, "you stop being preoccupied with the needs of your body and you can start appreciating the subtler things."

Few situations make you appreciate the subtler things more than military survival training. As a member of Army Special Forces (the Green Berets), I was often a student—and sometimes an instructor—of survival training in every imaginable terrain and climate. I've consumed rattlesnakes, ants, scorpions, alligators, rats, and gill-netted, trapped, speared and hooked countless varieties of fish from Alaska to Central America to Asia. One of the things I've discovered along the way is that life itself is nothing but a matter of survival. It is *how* we survive that truly matters, as we are only on this earth a mere eye blink before we move on.

During one of my first experiences with military survival training, a team of us dropped into Washington's Puget Sound, each equipped only with a helmet, a knife, and a parachute. We swam to the nearest uninhabited island where we split up to better avoid squads of fellow soldiers whose mission it was as the "enemy" to catch us and confine us in a "POW camp."

As I had grown up hunting and fishing the Ozarks, I not only survived, I *thrived*. The first thing I did was erect a well-camouflaged crawl-in shelter with the parachute canopy. Then I broke down parachute shroud lines for fishing lines and bow strings and a gill net. After that came the best part—hunting, fishing, and gathering.

I discovered a cherry tree ripe with fruit, a patch of "skunk cabbage," and fields of dandelion greens. The sea that surrounded the island was a virtual larder. Just at dawn each morning, before the "enemy" awakened, I slipped down to remote beaches to harvest crabs and snails and check my gill net for fish.

There was no eating anything raw either. I boiled everything in my helmet, mixing the ocean bounty with fresh greens and adding some seawater for seasoning. Sand crabs eaten shells and all taste a lot like peanut butter and crackers. The fish were delicate and fine and much prized. However, to my surprise, I discovered the real delicacy to be the big snails I found crawling around in their shells on rocky seashores.

I didn't realize what a cultured life I was living in the woods while surviving until years later in Paris, France. I had volunteered for Operation *Desert Storm*, the first Iraqi war, serving overseas as First Sergeant for a military police company. After the war ended quickly, I spent the next six months leading a military law-and-order mission in Germany. My girlfriend Nita flew over from the United States. We married in Denmark, she becoming my third wife, and honeymooned in Paris.

I discovered escargot on the menu one evening in a "fancy French restaurant." One delicious bite and I burst into laughter, recalling how I had captured "escargot" years earlier in Puget Sound and ate them out of my helmet. I had dined as well while surviving in the woods as now in Paris paying a fortune for a meal.

Lord, survival is more than ministering to the physical self. Feeding the spiritual person is even more vital.

Fishing Tip: Use visual clues to put yourself on fish when fishing timber-strewn reservoirs with plenty of structure. Bass will stick to specific features like humps, channels, larger trees, deadfalls and isolated clumps of wood.

Happy is he that hath the God of Jacob for his help, whose hope is in the Lord his God.
—Psalm 146:5

HOPE

I caught an Otter floatplane at Nakina in Ontario, Canada, along with my grandson Cass and six old friends, and flew an hour further north to a large natural lake upon whose wilderness banks our primitive cabin was located. As we were the only party on the lake, we could shout or sing or run naked in the woods and only God and assorted bears, wolves, and pine squirrels would see or hear. The plane would return for us in a week.

Some days, it rained. Others, the sun shined. I paired up with Cass or one of my fishing buddies to fish for Northern Pike or walleye. Someone always caught a few nice walleye to golden brown in the skillet at the end of the day. I preferred angling for pike, a bigger, scrappier fish.

One day D and I went out for Northerns, tucking silver spoons or soft white grubs into flat dark pockets of water trimmed in lily pads and sprigged with needle grass that stuck up from the surface like spikes. We worked around felled logs, sticking-up boulders, and beaver dams. Once we spotted a muskrat swimming, and then a bald eagle eyed us from the top of a fir.

Morning mist burned away, and we looked across the lake, narrow at this point, and saw the log cabin all blond in the sun and perched above the little dock where the spare boat was tied. A gull swaggered across the decking, waiting for fish scraps.

"Did you hear the loon this morning?" D asked.

"I hear him every morning."

Water nibbled at the boat. Braided line hissed off the reels as we cast. Lures plopped when they landed in the water. The soft grind of the reels whispered. The sun burned straight overhead and brassy on the water, like reflecting into a mirror.

Most big fish hit when least expected, as though to catch the angler after boredom and routine have set in. The tip of my rod twitched once. Spoon hung up on a weed? Then the pike hit so hard it almost jerked the rod out of my hand.

I yelped in surprise and caught the rod before it got away. At the same time I sprang to my feet, precariously balancing myself as the boat rocked from side to side. The light rod bent almost to the snapping point, vibrating. Line burned off the drag as the fish made its strong run across the front edge of the weed bed. I played it, not daring to horse it.

The fish erupted from the dark depths in a furious display, gills rattling, head shaking in a desperate attempt to throw the lure. A sleek, long body of a fish, dark on top, the color of the lake, sparkles of silver on the sides, with a full pearly underbelly. Mouth of teeth like an Arkansas River gar or a Suwannee 'gator.

It was almost too big to fit into the landing net. I got it in finally, head first with its fluted wild tail beating the rim. I threw down the rod and used both hands on the net handle to heave the monster over the gunwale and dump it into the bottom of the boat.

Later, as the sun sank slowly in the west, bleeding into the water, I walked next to the lake and paused to listen to the loon. Most people think its cry is the loneliest sound in the world, like a plea or a supplication. I have heard it many times, in different places in Canada and Alaska. To me, it is the voice of the wilderness itself, a reminder of the beauty and precision and thought God put into His masterful creation.

I lifted my head and smiled at God. By this time I was a confessed Christian, and getting to be an old man. Aloud, I thanked Him for the wonderful life He had given me, as I often did these days, and for all His blessings. I also thanked Him for the hope of His promise of Heaven.

A few years ago, Sam Harris wrote a book called *The End Of Faith*, one of any number of recent bestsellers by atheists. "At some point," he predicted, "there is going to be enough pressure that it is just going to be too embarrassing to believe in God."

How horrendous it must be to believe that life is nothing more than the snap of your fingers in the grand scheme of things, that you appear from nothing and, in a comparative instant, will vanish into nothingness. It must indeed be bleak and brutish in the minds of human beings who, in denying God, see no designed purpose for creation and therefore have given up all hope.

I am so grateful, Lord, for the hope that You have given me. I know that one day I will live forever where there are meadows and forests and streams flowing, all presented through Your love for us.

> **Fishing Tip:** Go north for pike and walleye as soon as possible after the spring thaw when these magnificent fish begin to spawn.

And the people sat down to eat and to drink, and rose up to play.
—Exodus 32:6

HUMOR

"Man," as Joseph Addison noted in the 17th Century, "is distinguished from all other creatures by the faculty of laughter."

The Bible tells us there is "*A time to weep, and a time to laugh...*" (Ecclesiastes 3:4)

Why else would God create humankind except that He have a sense of humor? I always supposed He laughed with us—and undoubtedly *at* us as well.

D and I, army buddies, have remained friends and fishing/hunting partners for nearly thirty years. Whenever we go fishing, I use light spinning gear with three- or four-pound line. D arms himself with a pole stiff enough to pry a Buick out of a bog and line stout enough to tow it back to the highway. I call it his "carp pole." He jerks the bottom out of a pond every time he sets a hook. All of which makes him perfect comic fodder for the campaign I've waged at his expense for years.

As a freelance writer/journalist, I frequently publish articles with fishing and hunting magazines. Right out of nowhere in many of the pieces I skillfully insert some reference to D's "carp pole." I once wrote a crime article for *True Detective* and talked about the body being discovered in "carp-infested waters." I penned fan letters to D postmarked from all over the world, mailed by friends of mine, in which each asked his advice on the catching and proper preparation of the bottom feeders. In some circles, D and his carp pole have become almost legendary, the mention of which is sufficient to break crowds into gales of laughter.

Fortunately, D also has a sense of humor.

He and I were bass fishing from the dock at my Lake Fort

Gibson ranch. As usual, I was casting with a light crappie rig when I hooked a monster that required nearly a half-hour of careful play before I got it to the surface and saw that it was a carp weighing at least thirty pounds. I had foul-hooked it in the thick flesh forward of its dorsal.

We didn't have a net with us big enough to land it. Thinking quickly, D grabbed a folding lawn chair. I steered the tiring behemoth close to the dock, and D scooped it up with the lawn chair.

Not only that, he posed for a photograph with the carp in the chair. Imagine the mileage I'm going to get with *that* photo.

God, it feels so good to laugh and have fun. In Your infinite wisdom, I think You must have realized that, life sometimes being difficult, mankind needed a way to offset the hard times. You therefore gave us humor and laughter.

Fishing Tip: Carp are terrific fighters, especially since they grow to spectacular sizes in many lakes and river. Try them for excellent sport, using for bait the following concoction: Slightly moisten a batch of Wheaties, add a little flour and then mix it with honey until it adheres in dough balls. Carp make delicious eating when prepared properly.

> *And Simon answering said unto him, Master, we have toiled all the night, and have taken nothing; nevertheless at thy word I will let down the net.*
> —Luke 5:5

PRIORITIES

I'm captivated by the works of Shakespeare. In *Troilus and Cressida,* he wrote, "The heavens themselves, the planets, and this centre observe degree, priority, and place...in all line of order." What does Shakespeare have to do with God and lessons learned in fishing? For one thing, he wrote about priorities, about what happens to people when they forget what is most important and descend into bitter irony. God wants us to avoid such traps by setting our priorities right, with His guidance. God has been teaching me ever since I was a kid to take easy that which is meant to be taken easy and use my energy for matters that really count.

Fishing, for example. Fishing is a medium by which I have learned never to take myself and life too seriously.

Kathy's uncles Bob and Richard Deatherage were obsessed with landing a trophy steelhead trout. Kathy was my second wife. For more than a decade the two brothers had flailed Michigan waters attempting to take a really big steelhead. They netted a few small ones, but nothing to write home about. Steelhead are apparently cunning, wary, finicky, and extremely difficult to catch.

One spring I drove to Michigan to fish with them. Bob and Richard attacked the trout stream with an intensity usually reserved for grave matters such as fighting off housebreakers or doing your income taxes. I baited a line, tossed it into deep water, and lay down on the grass with rod-and-reel across my chest to take a long nap in the sunshine.

"You'll *never* catch a steelhead like that," the Deatherages said, laughing.

I was relaxed and enjoying it. Priorities, right?

A jerk on the rod awoke me about an hour later. I scrambled to my feet and played in my first-ever steelhead while Bob and Richard gaped. It weighed over eleven pounds, a trophy.

"You have to hold your mouth right," I advised, recalling how my Paw used to say the same thing to me.

It just goes to show, on a minor level, how all the good things in life come through the setting of proper priorities.

Almighty Creator, I trust that You will ever establish in me priorities to light the path for others to come unto You.

Fishing Tip: In trout fishing, bigger isn't always better. Miniature swimming minnow lures (1/8 to 1/32 oz) on a light spinning outfit will often produce results when bugs and flies fail.

> *For there is no restraint to the Lord to save by many or by few.*
> —1 Samuel 14:6

SELF-CONTROL

My sons David and Michael were SCUBA-diving with me in Dominica, an island off the South American coast. The water was like polished crystal with visibility of more than one hundred feet. Amazing waters with even more amazing aquatic life swarming teeming around black coral reefs. Angel fish as big around as the mouths of barrels, puffers, yellow-striped clown fish, grouper, jack, and yellowtail. It was like swimming in the Sea World aquarium.

I chased schools of fish along the underwater stream beds, using only my fins with my arms flat along my sides, thrusting and winding as fast and hard as I could until the stream bed ended at the drop-off of a sheer underwater cliff. The water was so clear that it was like I propelled myself over the cliff into air and began *flying*.

After the diving, we sometimes caught fish in the harbor. The cook at dive headquarters served them fried golden brown or baked. Life didn't get much better.

One afternoon we dived on an old shipwreck, a freighter that was still well-preserved and teeming with sea life. The depth was about 120 feet, which meant a bottom time of only fifteen or twenty minutes in order to allow air reserve for stage decompression on the way back up the anchor rope. There was not a decompression chamber near enough to save us in the event we surfaced too rapidly and got the bends.

Bends are caused by nitrogen bubbles in the bloodstream. At depth, these compressed bubbles cause no problems. However, if a diver breathing compressed air attempts to surface without giving the air in his system time to disperse, the bubbles expand dramatically to cause intense joint pain, rupture of vital organs, and even death.

David and Michael, being considerably bigger men than I, consumed air at a much faster rate. We were all so enthralled with exploring the sunken freighter that Michael neglected to monitor his air pressure gauge. The first I knew he was in trouble was when he grabbed my elbow.

'He had less than five minutes' air remaining, which meant he would run out long before he could safely surface.

Throughout my years as a cop, soldier, and outdoorsman, God had instilled in me qualities of personal discipline and self-control, the ability to keep my head, as Kipling wrote, while all about are losing theirs. As calmly as I could, considering that my son was in trouble, I indicated to him that we would buddy-breath on the way up through my tank. Go slowly, I cautioned. Don't panic. Excitement burned up air at an accelerated rate.

Michael remained calm, even though we knew that I might not have enough air for both of us. Fish surged out of the way as I led us across the sea floor to the anchor. Michael tapped his mouthpiece, signaling that he had now expended his air supply. Bubbles ceased escaping his regulator.

I passed my mouthpiece to him, holding my breath while he took a gulp. We began slowly climbing the anchor rope, passing the air supply back and forth, stopping in stages along the way to allow ourselves time to decompress. I kept one hand clasped onto Michael's BC (buoyancy compensator) to keep us from inadvertently drifting apart.

It was nip-and-tuck whether we were going to make it or not. Air was being drained out of my tank at an alarming rate. *Don't worry,* I signaled Michael. *We'll make it.*

I saw the sheen of sunlight on the water surface above our heads, the long, dark underside of the dive boat. We were that close to making it when we ran out of air. I gave Michael the last breath from my tank. We had no choice now. We looked at each other, then held our breath as we finned our way to the surface.

Fortunately, we had sufficiently decompressed to a level that left only slight twinges and aches in our joints, like the onset of arthritis. We were lucky—and God was with us.

"I wouldn't want to be a fish," Michael exclaimed the moment we tasted fresh air.

Everything I have accomplished in life, Lord, is due to the discipline and self-control I have learned through You. Unfold within me Your will, Savior, and I will strive to fulfill it on the basis of these qualities.

Fishing Tip: One of the most wonderful destinations for winter fishing is Marathon in the Florida Keys. Offshore are dolphin, kingfish, and sailfish. Snapper, permit, mackerel and grouper inhabit nearby reefs. Contact Florida Department of Fish and Game for more details, or the Marathon Chamber of Commerce.

And in the and in thy seed shall all the families of the earth be blessed.
—Genesis 28:14

FAMILY

I read in Tolstoy's *Anna Karenina* how "all happy families resemble one another, but each unhappy family is unhappy in its own way." That described my family when I was growing up—"unhappy in its own way."

It wasn't that I was ever *personally* unhappy, not even while laboring in cotton fields or living hand-to-mouth in some shack, barn, or former chicken house. It was just that I never seemed to truly *belong*. Everyone said I was a strange little kid, always with a book in my back pocket and my head in the clouds dreaming of adventures yet to come, roaming the Ozarks all alone fishing and hunting, content with wild animals and wild country and God's raw nature. I never required much to be happy—an old cane fishing pole I cut myself, a quiet fishing hole. Even my beloved Paw, who often fished with me, referred to me as being a "little bit odd."

I *wanted* to belong. It just never seemed to happen. I have never felt truly at ease in crowds, even after I became a stage actor and public speaker. Likewise, I'm not quite comfortable with other Christians, having associated most of my life with soldiers, cops, cowboys, prize fighters, and other rough men. Fact is, after fourteen years as a cop I learned to trust a good roping pony more than most people.

I enlisted in the U.S. Navy when I was seventeen years old and never looked back. I served another 25 years in the U.S. Army after discharge from the navy, mainly as a Special Forces Green Beret. I married three times along the way, had two sons, and adopted Joshua. A wife left me every time I thought I might finally have a family.

Dianne's reasoning was that, as a cop, I had become hard

and tough and could never cry with the Oprah types on TV. For Kathy, it was because I was a freelance writer and sometimes spent weeks in Latin America or Asia covering wars for *Soldiers Of Fortune, Time/Life* and other publications. And Nita...? Well, Nita began sleeping with another man while I was still away in the first Iraqi war, Operation *Desert Storm,* even though we had just married.

I finally vowed that I was never meant to have a family. I roamed the globe seeking adventure and grist for my books and stories. I never intended to marry again. I always had girlfriends, but the instant one started hearing wedding bells... Well, thrice burned, thrice shy.

Still, I longed to belong somewhere. I actually prayed for God to send me someone special to keep.

God answers prayers, even from non-Christians. One Christmas, he sent me Donna Sue. I will never believe otherwise. She is a Christian and absolutely the best human being I've ever known. I was 54-years-old when we married. Donna Sue's previous two husbands had died, the first drowning while fishing on Keystone Lake, the second of cancer.

Finally, after so many years, I have a real home and a true family. Donna Sue's former in-laws and relatives adopted me. On a Thanksgiving, twenty or thirty people will show up for turkey, including my sons Michael and Joshua and their families, who live nearby. David is a medical doctor in California and can't always get away.

All the dreams I had as a kid have come true. I'm a successful writer. Donna Sue, her (our) son Darren, and I own GG Ranch where I have cattle and fine-blooded quarter horses. I live in a big two-story house. The ranch borders Lake Fort Gibson with its excellent fishing, and there are three ponds on the ranch, the largest of which is about an acre in size and stocked with largemouth bass.

Whenever we are hungry for fresh fish, I take my light spinning outfit or a fly rod, walk across the meadow, and catch three or four good bass. Donna Sue has them breaded and golden brown before they stop flopping.

God, you have given me far more in life than I deserve. I praise You for looking out for me all these years when I must have deserved less, for cultivating this lost sinner to bear Your fruit.

Fishing Tip: Catfish smell and even taste from a distance. A big mistake catfish anglers often make is assuming that a cut-up piece of bait is still doing its job when it's been in the water ten minutes. You will catch more fish if you change bait painfully often.

> *By which also ye are saved, if ye keep in memory what I have preached unto you...*
> —1 Corinthians 15:2

MEMORIES

I have found that as a man ages he begins to live less in what he will do (the future) and more in what he has done (the past). I suppose that is a natural progression from the point when one's life stretches out before him to when the most of one's life is behind him. Jesus told us that all things shall pass away, but God awarded us memory to anchor our lives in time and place and help us accept inevitable transitions in a wise and graceful manner.

"A fragrance in the air, a certain passage of song, an old photograph falling out from the pages of a book, the sound of somebody's voice in the hall...makes your heart leap and fills your eyes with tears," wrote Frederick Buechner.

The better our memories, the easier we pass into the next and succeeding stages of our lives. I have wonderful memories. Through God's teachings, I have learned not to harbor ill will or bitterness toward another human. Not even ex-wives, upon whom I can now look back on with fondness and even a certain amount of love.

First wife Dianne was Jewish with black hair and green eyes. A classic beauty. In my scrapbook are photos of her in the days when our two sons were little and we were happy. One photo shows me displaying a bass I have just caught. I'm wearing cut-off blue jeans, combat boots, and a big grin. Dianne took the photo.

Another photo shows Dianne on a beach at Keystone Lake frying fish over a campfire. She is laughing, while in the background in front of the tent David and Michael are playing in the sand.

Second wife Kathy was young, blond, petite, and pretty.

One year Kathy, son Joshua, and I rode "chicken buses" all over Mexico and went surf-fishing off the coast near Tampico. I see Kathy in short cut-off jeans, sea froth swirling around her legs. Joshua was about five. The first Spanish word he learned was *cabarone*. Shrimp. He couldn't get enough of them.

Third wife Nita was French, sultry and sexy. She had an affair with another man while I was off to the Arabian Gulf War. Nonetheless, I don't dwell on that. My best memories are those of a warm summer's day when we picnicked on Spring Creek and then went fly-fishing for perch.

God saved the best for last. Donna Sue is blond and pocket-sized with the most gorgeous eyes I have ever seen—and a soul to match. Absolutely the best human being I've ever known, a gift from God. I still see her in oversized wading boots standing in the middle of a New Mexico stream, fly-fishing for trout. Or at Valdez, Alaska, tied into a big silver salmon with her drag set too loose, cranking and cranking and getting nowhere while my son David and I were gabbing too busily to notice her distress.

Donna Sue and her son Darren influenced me to accept Jesus as my savior. Without them, I am certain to have died still questioning but never fully accepting. I will live and grow old and die with Donna Sue. Through her, God taught me to more fully appreciate my life as it was, as it is, and as it will be. Building memories for transition into old age and a new life in Heaven.

There is an old Gospel song that goes something like this: *God, if I make it to Heaven by the skin of my teeth, can I bring my own angel along...?*

Donna Sue is my angel.

I am so grateful, Lord, that You have awarded me memories of a full and good life. I pray, Lord, that all people whose lives I have touched will have generous memories of me—and of You.

Fishing Tip: While many fishermen go jigs for bluegill and other panfish, the absolute most perfect bait remains earthworms and night crawlers.

Afterword

When I started writing this book, I feared I could never fill its pages, that I hadn't sufficient stories to tell of God's wondrous ways of teaching. As I continued writing, however, the challenge was not in having too little to say but, instead, in having too much. I called publisher/editor Dan Case to report on my progress.

"How many words do you want?" I asked him.

"How many do you have?"

I told him.

"We may have to do another 'fishing' book," he exclaimed.

I hadn't even come to many of the lessons I was continuing to learn, such as compassion, forbearance, loyalty... Problem is, should I write a vignette on every single lesson God has taught me in his inimitable way—and is still teaching me—I would be at it for the rest of my life. The manuscript would have to be delivered to Dan in the back of a Ryder truck.

God is teaching not only fishermen, or writers, or golfers, or builders, or businessmen, or welders, or artists, or lawyers, or teachers, or... He is teaching every one of us, no matter who we are or what our avocation, if we but open our souls to Him. Since I happened to be an outdoors type, nature was the medium God chose to get me to listen.

God is speaking to you as well. You don't have to hear voices coming from a burning bush.

"We may our ends by our beginnings know," Sir John Denham wrote in the 17th Century.

I began by questioning, seeking. I'm sure I'll end up the same way. But as long as I continue to seek and question, I'm sure God will continue to teach.

Amen.

www.ingramcontent.com/pod-product-compliance
Lightning Source LLC
LaVergne TN
LVHW011357080426
835511LV00005B/327